THE
ELECTRONIC
UNIVERSITY

A Guide to
Distance Learning

D1604604

Published in cooperation with

**National University
Continuing Education Association**

Peterson's Guides

Princeton, New Jersey

Electronic University Network is a registered service mark
of Open Learning Systems, Inc., which has not participated
in the creation of this work.

The glossary is adapted in large part from the 1989 Office
of Technology Assessment Report to Congress: Linking for
Learning, A New Course for Education.

Library of Congress Cataloging-in-Publication Data

The Electronic University : a guide to distance
    learning.
        p.   cm.
    Includes index.
    ISBN 1-56079-139-X : $15.95
        1. Universities and colleges—United States—
Directories. 2. Universities and colleges—
Canada—Directories. 3. Distance education—
United States—Directories. 4. Distance
education—Canada—Directories. 5. Correspon-
dence schools and courses—United States—
Directories. 6. Correspondence schools and
courses—Canada—Directories.
L901.E49 1993
378.1'554'02573—dc20   93-28518
                                            CIP

Design and composition by Peterson's Guides

Printed in United States of America

10 9 8 7 6 5 4 3 2 1

CONTENTS

FOREWORD
KAY KOHL
EXECUTIVE DIRECTOR, NUCEA

Building on a long tradition, colleges and universities are now, more than ever, extending their resources beyond the physical borders of their campuses. Advanced communications technologies and telecommunications are enabling institutions to offer undergraduate, master's, and professional certificate programs to students in their homes and work sites.

Until now, no one volume has brought together the diverse instructional programs available electronically from individual universities or consortia of higher education institutions. The National University Continuing Education Association, in partnership with Peterson's, is proud to present *The Electronic University* as a guide to finding "nontraditional" ways of reaching "traditional" goals in higher education.

The Electronic University is a valuable tool for human resource directors, librarians, military personnel, and individuals. The publication describes various curricula available electronically from accredited, nonprofit, four-year colleges and universities. Because of the rapid expansion of such programs, no listing can purport to be comprehensive. The programs highlighted in this volume do evidence, however, the many ways in which higher education institutions are effectively utilizing modern instructional technologies to help students transcend significant time and geographic barriers to learning.

PHIL HAYS

Age: 43

Home: Vancouver, Washington

Institution: Colorado State University

Courses taken: Distance courses taken (via SURGE and Mind Extension University): continuous quality and productivity improvement, financial investments, marketing, finance, managerial economics, management accounting, business policy.

Academic achievement and goals: Hays has completed all M.B.A. course work with approximately two thirds taken via distance learning, and he is writing his M.B.A. professional paper. He holds a B.A. in international relations (University of Maryland) and an M.A. in Chinese studies (University of Michigan).

"I started taking distance learning courses when I lived in Fort Collins and was working on my M.B.A. at Colorado State. Through Colorado State's SURGE program for in-state students, I could view the classes on videotape. I could have driven over to the campus to attend the class in person, but my employer, Hewlett-Packard, made the materials available in its learning center. It was convenient and flexible. I avoided having to leave work to commute. Half the time I'd watch the lectures at the learning center; half the time I'd take them home.

"When Hewlett-Packard transferred me to Vancouver, I wasn't even thinking about finding time to finish my M.B.A. or finding a school that would accept my credits; I was more worried about getting my family situated in a new town. My new job was very exciting and, incidentally, was focused on developing programs to instill 'lifelong learning' into the work force. Hewlett-Packard is committed to creating a highly motivated and well-skilled work force—we have to, in order to compete in a global economy. Because my M.B.A. studies help me in my current job, HP provides 100 percent tuition reimbursement.

"So there I was in Vancouver, working long hours in my new job, when late one night I was flipping through the cable channels and saw one of my professors from Colorado State teaching a course in finance. It was 1:30 A.M., but I was so excited I even started taking notes! The next day I called my cable company, and they referred me to Colorado State, where I was told that, through Mind Extension University, the M.B.A. courses were offered over cable. I was lucky I was able to continue my studies virtually uninterrupted, with no loss of credits. Who would've thought that one part of getting my M.B.A. would be to learn how to program my VCR? I did goof up once, but Mind Extension sent me the tapes via express mail. In fact, you could purchase the whole set of a semester's class for about $175, and they would mail it two days after the classes were taped. The only friction was with my son, who claimed I was hogging the VCR when he wanted to play Nintendo! My wife, on the other hand, found the course interesting.

"A big advantage to distance learning was that as I watched students scrambling to take fast notes, I could pause and rewind. The trade-off, however, was the inability to interact with my classmates. Fortunately, my business policy professor required all distance learners to do a research paper and ten-minute videotape. He showed the class my tape and hooked up a conference call so I could field questions. It was great to get their feedback. After my M.B.A., I'm thinking of taking more classes—like Spanish—just because it's such a convenient way to learn."

Hays is a learning technology specialist for Hewlett-Packard Company.

IS DISTANCE EDUCATION RIGHT FOR YOU?

CHARLES E. FEASLEY
OKLAHOMA STATE UNIVERSITY

Before you can decide whether a distance program is right for you, you need to decide upon your educational goals. You may be interested in taking a single course for self-enrichment. Alternatively, your objective may be a higher education credential—either a certificate or a degree—to enhance your job prospects.

The latter situation raises a host of considerations. You will need to evaluate whether the sought-after credential will satisfy your career objectives as well as the specific certification requirements of a given profession. If your employer is providing tuition assistance, you will probably

Charles E. Feasley is director of Independent and Correspondence Study at Oklahoma State University. Feasley has published numerous articles on distance education for the International Council for Distance Education, NUCEA, the American Association of Higher Education, and the American Educational Research Association.

have to plan on earning a grade of C or better to qualify for such support. Once you have a clear understanding of your educational goals and how a distance education program might help you to realize those goals, it is important to review the course requirements carefully before registering. Often a program of study will require a fixed number of instructional modules, tests, mediated lessons, or interactions with the instructor.

Fortunately, distance education programs are becoming more numerous and more visible as employees and employers alike have come to recognize the importance of lifelong learning. Students appreciate the fact that distance education affords them access to outstanding faculty and library resources at institutions across the country.

While distance education offers many advantages, it is not for everyone. If you have difficulty planning and implementing long-term projects, then you may be wise to avoid self-pacing courses. If your employer or future graduate school is likely to equate educational quality only with a traditional on-campus higher education program, then you may not be able to secure the support needed to pursue your educational goals via a distance education program.

This book lists comparative characteristics of degree and certificate programs, such as admission requirements or enrollment restrictions, accreditation, method of course delivery, and on-campus components. Because each institutional listing includes full information on one or more contact persons, it is fairly easy to seek answers about concerns that are not addressed within specific institutional sections, such as the maximum number of prior credits that may be accepted from other institutions.

WHO ARE THE STUDENTS WHO LEARN BY DISTANCE EDUCATION?

Students who enroll in distance education tend to be over 25 years old and employed, and they generally have had some previous college experience. More than half are female. As a group, distance education students are highly motivated. Their course completion rate exceeds that of students enrolled in traditional, on-campus courses.

Successful distance learners are self-motivators who do not require regular reminders from the instructor or their classmates in order to meet deadlines. They have the discipline to establish a regular study schedule and set aside time daily or on specific days during the week for course work.

HOW ARE DIFFERENT TECHNOLOGIES USED TO HELP STUDENTS?

When you read about the technologies employed by various distance education programs, keep in mind that many students will select courses that utilize diverse technologies. This is partly because courses in certain content areas may only be available via a single delivery mode. For example, a course on computer-aided drafting may only be available to those willing to take a course that relies heavily on computer-assisted instruction. Also, whether a student chooses a given technology over another for learning will be influenced by time considerations and work and family obligations.

Often students' work environment will determine the technology they choose for distance education. Even though their preferred learning style might favor, say, videocassette courses, they may opt for courses that require a less comfortable learning approach, such as computer modem communication, because it figures importantly in the long-range plans of their employer. For instance, many students enrolled in master of library science programs are school librarians. They recognize that they must understand digitalized library systems in order to stay in the field, no matter how uncomfortable they may initially feel with the technology.

Chances are, your degree of comfort with computer-assisted instruction is greatly determined by how much you use computers at work or at home. Keep in mind that there are many different computer applications, including individual practice drills or simulations as well as model messages exchanged in real or delayed time. It is important to make certain that the software available for a given course will work with the computer you plan to use. An added consideration is whether you must have access to a computer printer in order to submit paper assignments or whether you may submit them by floppy disk or telecommunicated file.

The key variable with video/television courses is whether the instruction is live or recorded. A majority of U.S. households have the equipment to replay recorded videocassettes. In contrast, interactive live television is available in relatively few locations. Typically, interactive video sites are found in schools, businesses, and hotels. Other educational television delivery systems, such as instructional television fixed service (ITFS), microwave, and compressed video, are seldom available in homes. This means that students must travel to a campus or another public location to gain access to instructional video.

Audio is an attractive alternative for the adult student. Whether in the form of audiocassette, radio, or telephone, audio tends to be portable and low cost. When used in conjunction with videocassettes or still pictures, audio can be effective in many content areas.

CAREER COUNSELING AND THE DISTANCE LEARNER

When prospective distance learners have only vague ideas about what career direction to pursue, they may be well advised to take advantage of available career counseling services prior to enrolling in a specific program. Educational Information Centers, developed with federal and state funding, are located at public and private postsecondary educational institutions, public libraries, military bases, and prisons. These centers provide easy access to various career information resources in print, video, audio, and computer formats.

Such computerized database programs can be comprehensive, frequently updated, and personalized. This tends to make them too expensive for purchase by individuals. But the Educational Information Centers are likely to have one or more computer career counseling packages. One popular testing package employs a career choice decision-making model that helps users learn about: 1) the world of work; 2) some 450 specific occupations; 3) personal interests, abilities, experiences, and values; 4) educational choices; and 5) making life transitions. Another package begins with a self-assessment questionnaire on work-related values and activity preferences and enables the user to gather information about the skills and education required for some 200 occupations. Because of the interactive nature of these computer packages, it generally takes a student anywhere from three to five hours to complete a full sequence. Access to these computerized programs via computer modem and telephone lines may be

available but will be limited by the cost of direct telephone tolls.

ACADEMIC ADVISING AND THE DISTANCE LEARNER

Whether or not some career counseling precedes your decision to pursue a given distance education program, the availability of good academic advising is a critical consideration. Whenever possible, degree advisers usually try to have a face-to-face meeting with a beginning student. Although visits to remote sites are scheduled regularly, it may be quite a while before an adviser appears at a location near a potential student. Therefore you may choose to provide the adviser with information about your work experience and achievements as well as academic transcripts from previous institutions by means of mail, fax, or electronic mail. Some degree programs demand that requirements be satisfied with course-by-course matching. Still other institutions employ a portfolio assessment process that recognizes broad areas of competence. A number of institutions rely on computerized predictor tests to help students determine their readiness for particular equivalency tests or courses.

Electronic mail is used extensively these days by distance education students to interact with professors, program administrators, and other students. Exchanging computer messages and text files can be a quick way for you to obtain timely help on a troublesome section of a lengthy assignment. Exchanging fax messages can also provide rapid assistance but does not offer the flexibility of electronic mail.

Some institutions offer access to many services through a statewide computer network. Other colleges and universities rely upon the gigantic "network of networks," Internet, a global collection of 12,000 computer networks from over 40 countries that can communicate with each other. To get onto Internet, consult with your college or university. It is possible to connect to Internet in various ways and at various costs. Outside the university, people connect to Internet through computer centers in business and government; cooperative networks; commercial vendors and gateways; private entrepreneurs; and electronic bulletin boards, to name just a few of the options. To get onto Internet, you will need a computer, communications software, modem, and telephone line.

HOW SHOULD STUDENTS JUDGE COSTS?

In addition to comparing initial direct expenditures for course tuition and materials, you should also estimate subsequent costs for attending classes on campus (gas, oil, parking, etc.) or securing access to the equipment required for participating in distance classes. For instance, it may be necessary to buy a computer and a modem if you do not have access to them at work.

Depending on the institution, there may be a variety of financial aid programs for remote learners. Both federal and state government monies may be available to the distance learner. Courses that incorporate an interactive component will be more likely to qualify for aid. Military educational benefits are an important source of tuition assistance, as is tax-free employer-provided educational assistance. In addition, many colleges and universities offer deferred payment plans that can reduce the immediate burden on students who must finance their entire education themselves.

THE CONCLUSIONS ARE YOURS

To increase your likelihood of success in pursuing your educational goals, you should assess in advance your current capabilities, preferred learning styles, and expectations. Next, you must determine how you can best balance your educational goals with your work, family, and community commitments. Because technologies are evolving rapidly, it is essential to continually monitor distance education program options. This book should be considered an important resource that will grow with you over time.

KAREN FAGER

Age: 48

Home: Roseburg, Oregon

Institution: Portland State University

Courses taken: Fager completed 24 different courses, resulting in 72 credit hours via distance education. Courses included: accounting, marketing, management, statistics, international business, business economics.

Academic achievement: Fager received her B.A. in elementary education from Lewis & Clark College in 1967. In 1991 she earned her M.B.A. from Portland State via distance learning.

"Although I earned my degree in elementary education in 1967, upon graduation I compared an annual teacher's salary of $5200 to that of a department manager at JC Penney ($8300), where I'd been working part time, and decided to go into retail. Over the years I was also involved with small businesses on my own, and I always thought that when my children were older I'd like to earn my M.B.A.

"But then my husband was transferred to Roseburg, where there was no opportunity for an M.B.A. degree. That is, until Portland State's program came to Roseburg. I had heard about it in July 1988 while working at Umpqua County College in Roseburg. I acted quickly and started class in September. Since the distance learning classes were held at Umpqua twice a week from 6 to 9 P.M., I just stayed there all day on those days. We had exactly the same tests and instruction as the students in Portland, although our videotapes were one week delayed.

"We had no problems communicating with the instructors via toll-free numbers and voice mail. We knew their office hours, and they returned calls promptly. One drawback of the delayed videos was that we could not ask questions during the class, although usually the students in Portland would ask the same questions we might have.

"I graduated in 1991; there were three of us from Roseburg who graduated that year, and we all worked full time while earning our degrees. After I graduated, I became a class monitor for the program. Now I stay late at work and make sure the equipment is working and pass out tests. I can always find work in the office to do, but sometimes I will stay and watch a video if they're covering new material.

"The program now offers, through EdNet satellite-TV hookup, at least one opportunity for each instructor (usually early in the term) to talk to the whole group statewide. The video is one-way but has two-way audio to allow student questions on project requirements, term papers, etc.

"I've found the whole program enjoyable. Roseburg is a small community—I've seen lasting friendships and business relationships develop because of this program. It didn't matter that our class was so small, because for an M.B.A., no matter how large your class is, you break down into small groups anyway."

In 1993, seven students graduated from Portland State's site in Roseburg.

ALAN L. WEISER

Age: 58

Home: Rockville, Maryland

Institution: University of Maryland, University College

Courses taken: Via independent study: introduction to law, legal writing, legal research, torts, consumer protection law, litigation, contracts, legal ethics and law office management. On-site courses: advanced legal writing, advanced legal research.

Academic achievement: In addition to his paralegal document, which he received in May 1992, Weiser earned his M.A. in public administration in 1968 from the American University. His major fields of study were research and development, management, and information systems. He earned his B.S. in electrical engineering from the University of Rhode Island in 1956.

"I am deaf. I speak and read lips but do not sign. I became deaf in my senior year of undergraduate school in 1956. In 1968 I attended regular classroom classes and earned an M.A. with a 2.5 on a 3.0 scale.

"But from 1968 to 1990, when I entered the University of Maryland University College Paralegal Studies program, I did not attend any university classes for the simple reason that I could not hear the lecturers. I wanted to earn my paralegal document because I am interested in legal issues and, if I were to get laid off, like many in the defense industry, I wanted to be prepared to work in the field of law.

"Although the University of Maryland's Independent Learning (IL) Program may not have been designed to assist deaf students, it certainly served that purpose for me. I earned my paralegal document in May 1992, graduated with a 4.0 average for ten courses, and received the West Publishing Co. award for outstanding achievement in paralegal studies." (Weiser is pictured at left making his acceptance speech for the award.)

"When I first started my paralegal studies, I explained my hearing problems to the IL mentor. She offered to set up a communications modem so that I could ask questions and she could answer me. The personal computer modem, the Telecommunications Device for the Deaf (TDD), fax machines, E-mail, and telephone relay services are all excellent devices not only for the deaf but for those with a speech impairment. With the Americans with Disabilities Act requiring equal access for disabled persons, programs like the University of Maryland's should be well publicized.

"The college provided me with note-takers. Among the class requirements was a computer-intensive course in advanced legal research. We use computer workstations at the college to link into the on-line legal databases LEXIS and WESTLAW based in Ohio and Minnesota. Also, I found that a personal computer with word processing software, spell-checkers, and database management capabilities is almost a necessity for all paralegal students.

"I believe that the University of Maryland's Independent Learning Program provides an excellent opportunity for disabled students to gain a quality higher education without the many inconveniences and frustrations that accompany traditional classroom sessions."

Weiser is a department staff engineer at the Vitro Corporation.

COMPARING DISTANCE EDUCATION PROGRAMS

GARY E. MILLER
INTERNATIONAL UNIVERSITY CONSORTIUM

Many students who encounter distance education for the first time ask, not unreasonably, What is it all about? Perhaps the most important question for a prospective student is this: Is distance education a genuine educational experience? To put it bluntly: Is it the real thing?

Today advanced communications technologies make it possible for universities to serve adult students for whom distance is just one of several barriers to education, along with limited time, work and family commitments, and constrained financial

Gary E. Miller is associate vice president for program development at the University of Maryland University College, where he administers the development of open learning courses and technology-based distance education materials and chairs the Institute for Distance Education. He is also the executive director of the International University Consortium.

resources. Distance education affords students greater control over where they study, when they study, and, often, how long they take to complete a course. While the technologies are of relatively recent origin, the idea that universities should seek to serve students beyond the confines of the campus is by now a time-honored tradition in American higher education.

When shopping around for a distance education program, the potential distance learner should consider a number of important factors. For instance, while the diversity of technology allows students to match programs to their own learning styles, there are many practical issues that also must be taken into account. Are the courses available at times and in places the student is available? Is the program "portable"? For instance, can you take course materials with you when you travel or study at those odd hours that may be the only times you are free? Finally, is the necessary technology available?

Another consideration is the reputation of the institution. An increasing number of universities are extending specific programs statewide and nationally. If the institution is not one with which you are familiar, check to be certain that it is regionally accredited. In addition, try to ascertain the reputation of the specific program.

Prospective students should also seek to determine whether a given college or university is a full-service distance education institution. There is good reason for this. A student's success in distance education can depend to a surprising degree on support services such as academic advising, library access, and long-distance registration. Institutions with experience in distance education are most likely to have developed these services.

Also, consider the degree itself. Will you be able to apply previously earned credits toward the distance education program? Will credits earned toward distance education be applicable to your long-range educational plans? Can you earn the entire degree at a distance, or will you have to spend some time on campus? Will the degree be accepted by your employer or other institutions?

College and university distance education programs are offering vastly increased choice to students, but this abundance of offerings demands that students make informed decisions. Adult learners interested in distance education should resolve to be critical consumers. Call universities that offer programs of interest to you. Ask questions. And be sure you get the answers you need. Once you are satisfied that a particular program is the one for you, get involved and enjoy the new access—and empowerment—provided by distance education.

HOW TO USE THIS GUIDE

*T*he *Electronic University* profiles U.S. and Canadian institutions of higher education currently offering degree or certificate programs at a distance. The institutions included all meet the qualifications for membership in the NUCEA and must offer at least one professional certificate, baccalaureate degree, or professional degree principally off campus (the majority of course work can be completed at a distance) using primarily electronic means (telephone, video, computer) for course delivery and class interaction.

This definition of "distance education" does not include correspondence or independent learning courses that are based only on written interaction. For information on these types of distance education courses, refer to *The Independent Study Catalog,* published jointly by the NUCEA and Peterson's.

Institution profiles appear in alphabetical order in this guide and are broken down into the following groups of information to make searching in *The Electronic University* fast and easy.

General information—In this section you will find key facts and figures on the institution's experience in running distance education programs.

Institutional statement—A brief statement from each college or university gives you a quick overview of an institution's distance education plans and priorities.

Degree programs—Each degree or certificate program contains these elements:

- Area of study
- Degree or certificate granted upon completion
- Admission requirements
- Corporate or regional restrictions to program availability
- Media used to interact with professors and classmates
- Extent to which you may be required to spend time on campus
- Accrediting bodies recognizing that the program meets professional standards
- Contact information for program administrators

Individual courses—For those pursuing continuing education without a degree in mind, specific courses offered at a distance are listed in a separate index.

Subject and geographic indexes—These features allow you to find institutions offering programs or courses in your region and in each of 80 subject areas, from accounting to veterinary science.

SHEILA DEVOLLD

Age: 49

Home: Soldotna, Alaska

Institution: University of Arizona

Courses taken: Video courses taken in Anchorage: school library administration, collection development, foundation of libraries. Summer classes taken on-site in Tucson: children's literature, classification and cataloging, computer proficiency, reference, library management.

Academic achievement: In the summer of 1993, DeVolld successfully completed all requirements for her certificate in school librarianship. She is currently working toward her M.A. in library science.

"One of the reasons I chose the University of Arizona's program is that I could earn my school library certification first and also apply all those credits toward my master's.

"I was able to take video classes at the University of Arizona's satellite site in Anchorage. Unfortunately, Anchorage is 160 miles away! I was teaching elementary school full time, and twice a week, when school let out, I'd make the drive to Anchorage. It was dark, snowy, and sometimes 20 degrees below zero—but now I have my librarian certificate, and it was worth it.

"In Anchorage there were about 35 to 40 people in our class. We were located in the library of a junior high school and watched the classes from the University of Arizona campus on videotape. We had access to the professor via E-mail, fax, and the telephone, but we also had an instructional assistant in class to help us. She regularly consulted with the professor and acted as our mentor. If the class was unclear on something, the mentor stopped the video so we could discuss it. Also, when it came time for class discussion, rather than observing the on-campus class on the video, we would hold our own class discussion.

"By watching the videos, we felt as if we got to know the students in the Tucson classroom.

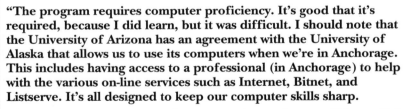

Because the program requires 12 credit hours to be earned on campus in Tucson, we also had the opportunity to meet them when we attended the summer school.

"The program requires computer proficiency. It's good that it's required, because I did learn, but it was difficult. I should note that the University of Arizona has an agreement with the University of Alaska that allows us to use its computers when we're in Anchorage. This includes having access to a professional (in Anchorage) to help with the various on-line services such as Internet, Bitnet, and Listserve. It's all designed to keep our computer skills sharp.

"I'm getting very accustomed to *extremes* in weather conditions—living in Alaska year-round and attending summer school in the desert!"

GLOSSARY OF ELECTRONIC MEDIA TERMINOLOGY

While many electronic media terms, such as diskette, fax, and on-line, are used increasingly in daily life, there are several very specific applications of electronic communications technology commonly used in distance education that require definition for the average nontechnical person. Here are some of them:

Addressable converter

A device connected to a television set that allows cable television operators to turn on or block individual subscriber access to pay-per-view services.

Amplifiers

Electronic devices, spaced at intervals (cascaded) throughout a cable television system, used to boost the strength of the cable signal as it passes from the headend to the subscriber. In coaxial cable systems, amplifiers are needed approximately every 1,500 feet.

Analog communication

A communication format in which information is transmitted by modulating a continuous signal, such as radio wave. *See also* Digital communication.

Asynchronous communication

Two-way communication in which there is a time delay between when a message is sent and when it is received. Examples include electronic mail and voice systems.

Audio bridges

Electronic devices that connect and control multiple telephone lines for audio and data applications, allowing many callers to be connected as a group simultaneously. Used for audioconferencing.

Audioconferencing

An electronic meeting in which participants in different locations use telephones to communicate simultaneously with each other.

Audiographics

An advanced computer application in which computer interaction is augmented by two-way, real-time audio communication. Audio, data, and graphics are shared over regular telephone lines, allowing users in different locations to work on the same application simultaneously.

Bandwidth

The width of frequencies required to transmit a communications signal without undue distortion. The more information a signal contains, the more bandwidth it will need to be transmitted. Television signals, for example, require a bandwidth of three million hertz (cycles per second), while telephone conversation needs only 3,000 hertz.

Bit (binary digit)

The smallest unit of information a computer can use. A bit is represented as a "0" or a "1" (also "on" or "off"). A group of eight bits is called a byte. Bits are often used to measure the speed of digital transmission systems.

Bitnet

An academic and research computer network that stores and forwards messages sent between users.

Bulletin board service (BBS)

A computer service that allows remote users to access a central "host" computer to read and post electronic messages. Communication is usually asynchronous.

Coaxial cable

Shielded wire cable that connects communications components together. It is commonly used in cable television systems because of its ability to carry multiple video (or other broadband) signals.

Codecs

The abbreviated form of "coder-decoder." Electronic devices that convert and compress analog video signals into digital form for transmission and convert them back again when they reach their destination.

Compact disc read-only memory (CD-ROM)

An optical storage system for computers that allows vast amounts of data, text, and images to be stored and retrieved off the disc. New data cannot be stored, and the disc cannot be erased for reuse. Although CD-ROMs look like music discs, they can only be used with a computer equipped with a CD-ROM drive.

Closed-circuit television

A system using coaxial cable, microwave transmissions, or telephone lines to allow audio and visual interaction within a building or small network of connected sites.

Compressed video

A video signal requiring less information to transmit than broadcast-quality or full-motion video. Digital technology is used to encode and compress the signal. Picture quality is generally not as good as full-motion; quick movements often appear blurred.

Computer conferencing

This describes an ongoing computer conversation with others in different locations. Conferencing can be done in "real time," so that messages appear as they are being keyed, or it can be "asynchronous," which means the complete message is keyed and then stored for later use by the receiver or sender.

Digital communications

A communications format used with both electronic and light-based systems that transmits audio, video, and data as bits ("1s" and "0s") of information (see Bit). Codecs are used to convert traditional analog signals to digital format and back again. Digital technology also allows communications signals to be compressed for more efficient transmission.

Digital video interactive (DV-I)

A system that combines audio, data, and limited-motion video on an optical disc. DV-I will run on a personal computer, allowing the user to control interactive programs.

Downlink

An antenna shaped like a dish that receives signals from a satellite. Often referred to as a dish, terminal, earth station, TVRO (television receive only).

Downstream

The direction a signal travels as it moves from the transmitting (origination) site to the receiving sites.

Electronic blackboard (or graphics tablet)

A computer device resembling a normal pad of paper that users draw or write on. The blackboard converts hand-drawn images into digital information that can be used and displayed by a computer.

Electronic bulletin board

An electronic mail box that allows all people involved in a given subject to send public messages and retrieve information via electronic mail.

Electronic mail

More often called E-Mail, this term refers to the use of a modem to send messages and documents over telephone lines to a receiving computer.

Facsimile machine (fax)

A telecopying device that electronically transmits written or graphic material over telephone lines to produce "hard copy" at a remote location.

Fiber optics

Hair-thin, flexible glass rods that use light signals to transmit audio, video, and data signals. Signals can be sent in either analog or digital format. Fiber optic cable has a much higher capacity than traditional copper or coaxial cable and is not as subject to interference and noise.

Freeze frame

One method of transmitting still images over standard telephone lines. A single image is transmitted every 8 to 30 seconds. Also referred to as slow scan.

Frequency

The number of times per second an electromagnetic wave completes a cycle. A single hertz (Hz) is equivalent to one cycle per second.

Full-motion video

A standard video signal that can be transmitted by a variety of means, including television broadcast, microwave, fiber optics, and satellite. Full-motion video traditionally requires six MHz in analog format and 45 Mbps when encoded digitally.

Headend

In a cable television system, the headend is the central transmission office from which programming is distributed to subscribers.

Instructional Television Fixed Service (ITFS)

A band of microwave frequencies set aside by the U.S. Federal Communications Commission exclusively for the transmission of educational programming. Allows broadcast of audio, video, and data to receive sites located within 20 miles. Receive sites require a converter that changes signals to those used by a standard television set.

Integrated Services Digital Network (ISDN)

An end-to-end digital network that will allow users to send voice, data, and video signals over the same line simultaneously. Narrowband services now in operation give users up to 24 channels to send voice and data information, with a combined capacity of up to 1.544 Mbps. In the future, broadband services available over a public ISDN are expected to offer full-motion video services as well.

Internet

This is the increasingly popular global network of more than 12,000 computer networks that allows computer conferencing and access to databases among approximately 1,800 "news groups." In the U.S.,

Internet is managed in large part by the National Science Foundation.

Limited-motion video
See Compressed video.

Microwave
High-frequency radio waves used for point-to-point and omnidirectional communication of audio, data, and video signals. Microwave frequencies require direct line-of-sight to operate; obstructions such as trees or buildings distort the signal.

Modem (modulator/demodulator)
A device that converts digital computer signals into analog format for transmission.

Real-time communication
Two-way simultaneous communication, as opposed to asynchronous.

Satellite television
This refers to courses that are broadcast, usually live, by an electronic signal sent to a satellite orbiting the earth and then retrieved by a satellite dish. The satellite dish broadcasting the program is called an "uplink," and the receiving dish is called a "downlink."

Slow scan
See Freeze frame.

Switched network
A type of system in which each user has a unique address (such as a phone number) that allows the network to connect any two points directly.

Teleconferencing
A general term for any conferencing system using telecommunications links to connect remote sites. There are many types of teleconferencing, including videoconferencing, computer conferencing, and audioconferencing.

Television receive only (TVRO)
Satellite dishes capable of reception only.

Touch screen
A computer screen that allows data to be entered by using a specialized pen to write on the screen or by making direct physical contact with the computer screen.

Transponder
The electronic equipment on a satellite that receives signals from an uplink, converts the signals to a new frequency, amplifies the signal, and sends it back to earth. Satellites are usually equipped with 12 to 14 transponders.

Uplink
A satellite dish that transmits signals up to a satellite.

Upstream
The direction a signal travels as it moves from a receive site back to the site of the original transmission. Used especially in two-way cable television systems.

Videoconferencing
Linking two or more locations by two-way video, allowing all participants to see each other simultaneously.

Videodisc
A record-size CD that can store data, text, still images, and full-motion video images.

DISTANCE DEGREE CONSORTIA AND NETWORKS

The institutions profiled in *The Electronic University* are often affiliated with various distance education organizations in order to make their programs more accessible to a broader audience and to expand the offerings they can make to their own students.

These organizations generally fall into two categories: consortia—colleges and universities that cooperate in the creation and dissemination of courses; and networks—companies that use communications technologies to provide access to programs at participating institutions.

Please note that this brief list is not intended to be a complete guide to the many organizations active in distance education. It is, rather, intended to give you some background information on the consortia and networks mentioned in the body of this guide and enable you to contact them directly if you have further questions.

Also note that you will see institutions listed as consortia or network affiliates that are not included in the body of the guide. This is because those institutions have not indicated to us that they confer a degree or certificate primarily via distance education or are otherwise not qualified for inclusion in this directory. (See How to Use This Guide for a complete explanation of the criteria for inclusion.)

One final point: An institution's participation in a given consortium may mean that it receives courses at a distance and offers credit for them but does not grant the degree earned as a result of their completion. Another institution in the consortium may grant the degree earned. Because there are many complex inter-institutional arrangements like this in distance education, you are encouraged to read each program's profile carefully and contact each institution directly to get the details you need to make your final decision.

AG*SAT

The Agricultural Satellite Corporation (AG*SAT) is a national consortium of land-grant institutions affiliating with other educational institutions, government, business, and industry to develop and provide responsive, high-quality and economical distance learning programs and services. Through the consortium, primary emphasis is placed on educational and informational programs and services related to agriculture, food and nutrition, natural resources and the environment, communities, families, and youth.

Programs and services are offered through emerging technological capabilities and are aimed at diverse audiences. AG*SAT, focusing on explicit learning objectives, uses the latest and most appropriate networked communication technologies and draws upon the best and most effective subject matter specialists and information resources to share knowledge and content with members of the consortium and their clientele. Academic, extension, and research programs are offered intra- and interstate, regionally, nationally, and internationally, depending on need and efficiency of distribution.

AG*SAT's land-grant affiliates include Clemson University, Colorado State University, Cornell University, Delaware State College, Iowa State University, Kansas State University, Louisiana State University, Michigan State University, Mississippi State University, North Carolina A&T University, North Carolina State University, Ohio State University, Oklahoma State University, Oregon State University, Pennsylvania State University, Purdue University, Rutgers–The State University of New Jersey, South Dakota State University, Tennessee State University, Texas A&M State University, Tuskegee University, Utah State University, Virginia State University, Virginia Tech, Washington State University, West Virginia University, University of Arizona, University of Arkansas, University of California, University of Connecticut, University of Delaware, University of Florida, University of Georgia, University of Idaho, University of Illinois, University of Kentucky, University of Maine, University of Maryland–Eastern Shore, University of Minnesota, University of Missouri–Columbia, University of Nebraska–Lincoln, University of Nevada–Reno, University of New Hampshire, University of Tennessee, University of Wisconsin–Madison, and University of Wyoming.

To learn more about AG*SAT, call AG*SAT Director Randy Bretz at 402-472-3611 or write to AG*SAT, 1800 N. 33rd St., P.O. Box 83111, Lincoln, NE 68501.

ELECTRONIC UNIVERSITY NETWORK

The Electronic University Network (EUN) pioneered the use of computers and modems for college study. It has been serving students on-line since 1983, providing undergraduate and graduate credit courses and degree programs to nearly 12,000 students.

Institutions offering distance degree programs via EUN include the California Institute of Integral Studies (Ph.D. in Integral Studies), Heriot-Watt University (M.B.A.) and Rogers State College (A.A., A.S.). EUN also offers about 60 undergraduate courses that earn college credit by examination and enable students to earn an associate or bachelor's degree from an external-degree-granting college. Credits earned by examination are accepted by 2,500 U.S. college and universities.

EUN is the exclusive provider of higher education on America Online, a national public computer network with about 250,000 subscribers. EUN on America Online provides a virtual campus for class meetings, study, research, instructor/student conferences, and student life. The campus includes academic areas, an admissions office, a registrar's office, a finance office, academic counseling, a student union, a library, and a continuing education center. America Online supports IBM, Macintosh, and Apple II users with software and technical assistance.

Prospective students who have a computer and modem may visit the Electronic University Campus by requesting free America Online software by calling 800-225-3276 or may write or call the Electronic University, 1977 Colestin Rd., Hornbrook, CA 96044; telephone: 503-482-5871. Electronic mail: Internet, EUN-

Learn@aol.com; America Online, EUN-Learn.

INTERNATIONAL UNIVERSITY CONSORTIUM

The International University Consortium (IUC) is a cooperative organization of colleges, universities, and educational communications agencies in the U.S., Canada, and around the world that have joined together to develop and use media-assisted course materials in a variety of adult degree programs. It was formed in 1980 by University of Maryland University College and Maryland Public Television, IUC has been an innovator in distance and open learning since its inception. Today it is administered on behalf of its members by University of Maryland University College.

IUC offers institutions access to a broad range of courses. Through IUC membership, institutions can license individual courses to integrate into other adult degree programs. Institutions participate in course development and can use IUC courses as the core of several upper-division degree concentrations. A solid core of four division IUC courses can be organized around general education requirements, helping to serve students with the foundation for meaningful comprehensive education. The IUC range of upper-division course offers a solid degree-completion core in four areas of concentration: general management, health-care management, liberal studies, and American studies.

IUC also offers a collection of print-based courses provided by IUC member institutions or other IUC members to adapt for their own use. This major collection gives IUC members access to worldwide open and distance education resources.

To learn more about IUC, call John Strain at 301-985-7811 or write to International University Consortium, University of Maryland University College, University

Blvd. at Adelphi Rd., College Park, MD 20742-1660.

MICHIGAN INFORMATION TECHNOLOGY NETWORK, INC.

MITN is a nonprofit partnership of education, government, and business created to foster the education and training of Michigan's citizens through the use of distance learning. MITN's Business Network makes graduate courses and seminars available to fee-paying sites via satellite television.

MITN offers graduate degrees in 15 disciplines, broadcasting over 300 courses annually. The master's degrees offered through MITN include business administration (M.B.A.); civil engineering; computer engineering; computer science; electrical engineering; engineering management; hazardous waste management; health physics; industrial and systems engineering; management of technology; manufacturing systems engineering; materials science; mechanical engineering; software engineering; and systems engineering.

Network members include Michigan State University, National Technological University, and Western Michigan University.

For more information, call Sara Gozmanian at 517-336-1321 or write to MITN, 4660 S. Hagadorn Rd. #230, East Lansing, MI 48823.

MIND EXTENSION UNIVERSITY

ME/U is a network that provides distance programs of study through cable and satellite television as well as videotape distribution.

All credit courses are provided by fully accredited universities, including California State University at Long Beach, Colorado State University, Emporia State University, George Washington University, Governors State University, Kansas State University, New Jersey Institute of Technology, Oklahoma State University, SUNY/Empire State College, Pennsylvania State University, University of Arizona,

University of California at Berkeley, University of California at Santa Barbara, University of Maryland University College, University of New Orleans, University of Oklahoma, University of South Carolina, Utah State University, Washington State University, and Western Michigan University.

Undergraduate degree programs accessible through ME/U are provided by member institutions in the National Universities Degree Consortium (see subsequent listing) and include the Agriculture, Animal Sciences, and Industry: Animal Products Option Completion Degree granted by Kansas State University, the Interdisciplinary Social Science Degree granted by Kansas State, the B.A./B.S. Management Completion Degree granted by the University of Maryland University College, and the Social Science Completion Degree granted by Washington State University.

Graduate degree programs accessible through ME/U include the Master's of Business Administration granted by Colorado State University, the Master of Arts in Education and Human Development granted by George Washington University, and the Master of Library Science degree granted by the University of Arizona. A Graduate Certificate in School Librarianship and a Correspondence Certificate in School Librarianship are also available and are granted through the University of Arizona.

For specific course or degree program information, call ME/U at 800-777-6463 between 7 a.m. and 11 p.m. (eastern time) or write to Mind Extension University, 9697 East Mineral Ave., P.O. Box 3309, Englewood, CO 80155-3309.

NATIONAL TECHNOLOGICAL UNIVERSITY

[See the full profile of NTU detailing all of its programs on page 49.]

Member universities in NTU include Arizona State University, Boston University, Colorado State University, Columbia University, Cornell University, George Washington University, Georgia Institute of Technology, GMI Engineering and Management Institute, Illinois Institute of Technology, Iowa State University, Kansas State University, Lehigh University, Michigan Technology, New Jersey Institute of Technology, New Mexico State University, North Carolina State University, Northeastern University, Oklahoma State University, Old Dominion University, Purdue University, Rensselaer Polytechnic Institute, Southern Methodist University, University of Alaska, Fairbanks, University of Arizona, University of California, Berkeley, University of California, Davis, University of Colorado at Boulder, University of Delaware, University of Florida, University of Idaho, University of Illinois at Urbana-Champaign, University of Kentucky, University of Maryland College Park, University of Massachusetts at Amherst, University of Minnesota, University of Missouri–Rolla, University of New Mexico, University of Notre Dame, University of South Carolina, University of Southern California, University of Tennessee, Knoxville, University of Washington, and University of Wisconsin–Madison.

NATIONAL UNIVERSITIES DEGREE CONSORTIUM

NUDC was established in 1990 to offer bachelor's degree programs in a flexible, off-campus format suitable for adult and part-time students. Members use the Mind Extension University distribution network (see previous listing) to deliver courses.

Members include California State University, Long Beach, Colorado State University, Kansas State University, Oklahoma State University, University of Maryland University College, University of New Orleans, University of Oklahoma, University of South Carolina, Utah State University, and Washington State University.

TRIBAL COLLEGE CONSORTIUM

The TCC consists of three colleges that serve the Native American community in Montana and share courses through a telecommunications exchange. TCC members include Rocky Mountain College (Billings), Fort Peck Commmunity College (Poplar), and Little Big Horn College (Crow Agency).

For more information, call Richard Widmayer at 406-657-1020 or write to Tribal College Consortium, c/o Rocky Mountain College, Billings, MT 59012.

WESTERN COOPERATIVE FOR EDUCATIONAL TELECOMMUNICATIONS

The Western Cooperative, part of the Western Interstate Commission for High-er Education (WICHE), was founded in 1989 and has emerged as a leading voice in the increased use of quality distance learning through new technologies. The 150-member cooperative represents a partnership of states, institutions, networks, public broadcast stations, school districts, and telecommunications concerns and has been instrumental in evaluating distance learning programs and paving the way for an expanding number and range of programs that meet quality standards.

For more information, call Mollie McGill at 303-541-0233 or write to WICHE, P.O. Drawer P, Boulder, CO 80301-9752.

SHARON ANGLE

Age: 39

Home: Exmore, Virginia

Institution: Old Dominion University

Courses taken: Earned her B.S. in nursing by transferring liberal arts requirements from her local community college and completing 300/400-level nursing courses and required nursing electives (approximately 60 credit hours) via interactive television.

Academic achievement: In August 1993, Angle successfully completed all requirements for her M.S. in nursing with a primary focus in administration and a secondary focus in critical care.

"Distance learning wasn't just a convenient option for me; it was the *only* way I could earn my B.S. and M.S. degrees. Having attended a diploma school, I was already working as a registered nurse. I wanted to earn my B.S., but the ODU campus is one-and-a-half hours away in Norfolk. Not only that, but I'd have to take the Chesapeake Bay Bridge-Tunnel, which costs $20 in round-trip tolls. That, plus gas, becomes very expensive.

"About ten years ago I tried moving to a university town in North Carolina so I could work full time and attend the university there. But it was very difficult for me after I'd been working in the profession for several years to be back in classes with college students who were just beginners. It was also tough to arrange my work schedule to fit into the spare time of a traditional college student.

"After a couple of years I moved back to the Eastern Shore. I was working as a nurse manager in a skilled-care facility when I learned about ODU's new program. They allowed me to 'challenge out' of certain courses if I already knew the subject matter. (Now ODU offers an 'abridged edition' course for working RNs.) The quality of the program was wonderful, and the cooperation of the area hospitals made the whole process very workable. Most hospitals set up satellite sites so that even people in Norfolk could work up until the last minute and run down the hall to class instead of having to drive to the campus. They are now going statewide and televising in Charlottesville and other areas of Virginia.

"The quality was excellent. We could see everybody in the Norfolk location, and the camera could be turned to pan the room. They couldn't see us, but they could hear us. To ask a question, we'd push a button to dial into the class, and our photo would flash on the screen. We also had a contact person at our hospital who acted as a coordinator, timekeeper, and collector for tests.

"This program is a great opportunity. It has increased my ability to do my job, and I have benefited professionally and financially."

Angle is employed in quality assessment and infection control at North Hampton Accomack Memorial Hospital in Nassawadox, Virginia.

PROGRAM PROFILES

ACADIA UNIVERSITY
WOLFVILLE, NOVA SCOTIA B0P 1X0, CANADA

Acadia University first offered a degree program via distance education in 1989. Total enrollment in distance education programs (1992–93): 100.

DEGREE PROGRAM

BUSINESS ADMINISTRATION

Certificate in Business Administration. First year of B.B.A. program—30 credit hours including accounting, introduction to business, and electives.

Requirements: High school diploma; if over three years out of school, no requirements.

Degree/Certificate Awarded: Postsecondary certificate.

Availability: Open to the public; regional.

Primary Method of Course Delivery and Response: Teleconferencing.

Accreditation: Institute of Canadian Banking, Purchasing Management Association of Canada.

For more information, contact: Mr. Terry Grignon, Coordinator of Credit Programs and Education Technology, Division of Continuing Education, Acadia University, Wolfville, Nova Scotia B0P 1X0, Canada; Telephone: 902-542-2201 Ext. 178; Fax: 902-542-3715; Internet: TGRIGNON@MAX.ACADIAU.CA.

INDIVIDUAL COURSES

Acadia University offers individual for-credit courses in: accounting (undergraduate); business/management (undergraduate); computer science (undergraduate); liberal arts/general studies (undergraduate); nursing (undergraduate); teacher education (graduate).

ARIZONA STATE UNIVERSITY
TEMPE, AZ 85287

Arizona State University first offered a degree program via distance education in 1982.
Total enrollment in distance education programs (1992–93): 3,290.

Arizona State University offers approximately 55 credit courses each semester via ITFS, cable, public television, and satellite. A complete master's degree in electrical engineering is offered, as well as noncredit courses and seminars. The ITFS network includes two public sites and 21 corporate locations. Arizona State offers courses nationwide via National Technological University.

DEGREE PROGRAM

ENGINEERING
Master of Science in Engineering. Graduate degree in electrical engineering. All courses necessary for the program are offered via technology.

Requirements: 3.0 GPA; bachelor's degree in related area.

Degree/Certificate Awarded: Master's—M.S.E.

Availability: Open to the public; local.

Primary Methods of Course Delivery and Response: ITFS; cable television; public television; satellite television.

For more information, contact: Elizabeth Craft, Director, Distance Learning Technology, Arizona State University, Box 872904, Tempe, AZ 85287-2904; Telephone: 602-965-6738; Fax: 602-965-1371; Internet: ICSEAC@ASUVM.INKE.ASU.EDU; Bitnet: ICSEAC@ASUACAD.

INDIVIDUAL COURSES

Arizona State University offers individual for-credit courses in: architecture and environmental design (undergraduate); computer science (undergraduate and graduate); criminal justice/law (undergraduate); engineering (undergraduate and graduate); liberal arts/general studies (undergraduate and graduate); nursing (undergraduate); teacher education (undergraduate).

ATLANTIC UNION COLLEGE
SOUTH LANCASTER, MA 01561

Atlantic Union College first offered a degree program via distance education in 1991.

Total enrollment in distance education programs (1992–93): 1,800.

Number graduating from distance programs (spring 1992): 20.

DEGREE PROGRAMS

GENERAL STUDIES
Associate Degree in General Studies. First three years (66 hours) of general core curriculum; five different emphasis areas.

Requirements: High school diploma or GED; 24 hours undergraduate credit/certificate; 2.5 GPA.

Degree/Certificate Awarded: Associate—A.A.

Availability: Open to a restricted group; national.

Primary Methods of Course Delivery and Response: Computer conferencing; electronic bulletin board; electronic mail.

For more information, contact: Robert Malin, Director, Electronic Distance Learning, Atlantic Union College, Box 1000, South Lancaster, MA 01561; Telephone: 508-368-2394; Fax: 508-368-2386.

GENERAL STUDIES
Certificate in General Studies. First-year college equivalent (24 semester hours) including required courses in humanities/social sciences, business, and computer programming.

Requirements: High school diploma; testing under Federal Pell Grant for those without diploma.

Degree/Certificate Awarded: Postsecondary certificate.

Availability: Open to the public (80 percent of enrollees are prison inmates); national.

Primary Methods of Course Delivery and Response: Computer conferencing; electronic bulletin board; electronic mail.

For more information, contact: Robert Malin, Director, Electronic Distance Learning, Atlantic Union College, Box 1000, South Lancaster, MA 01561; Telephone: 508-368-2394; Fax: 508-368-2386.

INDIVIDUAL COURSES

Atlantic Union College offers an individual for-credit course in: liberal arts/general studies (undergraduate).

BALL STATE UNIVERSITY
MUNCIE, IN 47306

Ball State University first offered a degree program via distance education in 1986. Total enrollment in distance education programs (1992–93): 1,229.

Number graduating from distance programs (spring 1992): 44.

Ball State University's distance education program addresses the educational needs of Ohio residents. The program delivers academic instruction to the workplace (hospitals, industries, schools); offers instructional programs on a flexible schedule; delivers pertinent information to a wide audience; and acts as a catalyst for better inter- and intra-institutional cooperation.

DEGREE PROGRAM

BUSINESS
Master of Business Administration. A magnified look at accounting, economics, finance, and operation techniques as they relate to management.

Requirements: Bachelor's degree; GMAT.

Degree/Certificate Awarded: Master's—M.B.A.

Availability: Open to the public; statewide.

Primary Method of Course Delivery and Response: Satellite television; Indiana Higher Education Telecommunications System.

Accreditation: American Assembly of Collegiate Schools of Business.

For more information, contact: Tamara Estep, Director, Graduate Programs, College of Business, Ball State University, Muncie, IN 47306; Telephone: 317-285-1931; Fax: 317-285-8818.

INDIVIDUAL COURSES

Ball State University offers individual for-credit courses in: accounting (undergraduate and graduate); business/management (undergraduate and graduate); high school advanced placement; liberal arts/general studies (undergraduate); nursing (undergraduate); teacher education (graduate).

BASTYR COLLEGE
SEATTLE, WA 98105

Bastyr College first offered a degree program via distance education in 1992. Total enrollment in distance education programs (1992–93): 20.

Bastyr is the only accredited college offering course work in natural health sciences and nutrition from a holistic perspective.

DEGREE PROGRAM

NATURAL HEALTH AND NUTRITION
Certificate. An academic course of study for interested laypeople, natural products industry employees, and health-care professionals.

Requirements: High school diploma or GED.

Degree/Certificate Awarded: Postsecondary certificate.

Availability: Open to the public; national.

Primary Methods of Course Delivery and Response: Audiocassette; telephone; videocassette.

For more information, contact: Russ Romans, Director of Continuing Education, Distance Learning, Bastyr College, 144 NE 54th Street, Seattle, WA 98105; Telephone: 206-523-9585; 206-527-4763.

INDIVIDUAL COURSES

Bastyr College offers individual for-credit courses in: allied health (undergraduate).

BOISE STATE UNIVERSITY
BOISE, ID 83725

Boise State University first offered a degree program via distance education in 1989.

Total enrollment in distance education programs (1992–93): 795.

Number graduating from distance programs (spring 1992): 22.

Distance education at Boise State University utilizes a variety of technologies, including asynchronous computer conferencing, ITFS and cablecast, and broadcast telecourses on PBS and via satellite. Boise State University is pioneering the use of on-line communication to deliver graduate and undergraduate courses.

DEGREE PROGRAM

INSTRUCTIONAL AND PERFORMANCE TECHNOLOGY
Master of Science in Instructional Performance and Technology. Prepares students for careers in instructional design, job performance improvement, human resources, training, and training management.

Requirements: Undergraduate degree; minimum 2.75 GPA; minimum score of 50 on MAT.

Degree/Certificate Awarded: Master's—M.S.

Availability: Open to the public; national.

Primary Methods of Course Delivery and Response: Asynchronous computer conferencing; audiocassette; on-line communication.

Accreditation: Northwest Association of Schools and Colleges.

For more information, contact: Joanne Fenner, Associate, Program Development, Instructional and Performance Technology, Boise State University, 1910 University Drive, Boise, ID 83725; Telephone: 208-385-1899; Fax: 208-385-4081.

INDIVIDUAL COURSES

Boise State University offers individual for-credit courses in: accounting (undergraduate); allied health (undergraduate); business/management (undergraduate); computer science (undergraduate); engineering (undergraduate); foreign languages (undergraduate); liberal arts/general studies (undergraduate); nursing (undergraduate); teacher education (undergraduate).

CALIFORNIA INSTITUTE OF INTEGRAL STUDIES
SAN FRANCISCO, CA 94117

California Institute of Integral Studies first offered a degree program via distance education in 1993.
Total enrollment in distance education programs (1992–93): 20.

An important aspect of integralism is the process of exploration and discovery. The California Institute of Integral Studies is committed to this perspective administratively as well as academically and seeks to create an institutional form and set of academic practices that express the insights and values of integral philosophy.

DEGREE PROGRAM

INTERDISCIPLINARY STUDIES
Interdisciplinary Doctoral Studies Program. An innovative approach to studying and researching transformative change in individuals, groups, and cultures.

Requirements: Master's degree.

Degree/Certificate Awarded: Doctorate—Ph.D.

Availability: Open to the public; national.

Primary Method of Course Delivery and Response: Electronic bulletin board.

On-Campus Component: One week; also experimental group with no residency.

Accreditation: Western Association of Schools and Colleges.

For more information, contact: Enrollment Manager, CIIS-School for Transformative Learning, 765 Ashbury St., San Francisco, CA 94117; Telephone: 415-753-6100 Ext. 263; Fax: 415-753-1169.

INDIVIDUAL COURSES

California Institute of Integral Studies offers an individual for-credit course in: liberal arts/general studies (graduate).

CALIFORNIA STATE UNIVERSITY, CHICO
CHICO, CA 95929

California State University, Chico, first offered a degree program via distance education in 1975.

Total enrollment in distance education programs (1992–93): 2,000.

Number graduating from distance programs (spring 1992): 30.

California State University, Chico, has been active in distance learning since 1975, when its ITFS/microwave system was started. A C-band uplink was installed in 1984, and a Ku-band uplink was installed in 1986. The school is one of the few institutions in the U.S. that has both C- and Ku-band uplink facilities located on its campus. It delivers a variety of courses and programs to northern California and locations across North America.

DEGREE PROGRAMS

COMPUTER SCIENCE
SEN—Satellite Education Network. Bachelor's and master's degree programs in computer science delivered live and interactively to corporate subscribers in North America via satellite.

Requirements: Same as for on-campus students.

Degree/Certificate Awarded: Bachelor's—B.S., Master's—M.S.

Availability: Open to corporate subscribers; national.

Primary Method of Course Delivery and Response: Satellite television.

Accreditation: Computer Science Accreditation Commission.

For more information, contact: Leslie J. Wright, Associate Dean, Regional and Continuing Education, California State University, Chico, Chico, CA 95929-0250; Telephone: 916-898-6105; Fax: 916-898-4020; Internet: LWRIGHT@OAVA.CSUCHICO.EDU.

LIBERAL ARTS/GENERAL STUDIES
ITFS—Instructional Television for Students. University courses delivered live and interactively via microwave. ITFS reaches 14 learning centers in northeast California.

Requirements: Same as for on-campus students.

Degree/Certificate Awarded: Bachelor's—B.A.

Availability: Open to the public; regional (northern California).

Primary Methods of Course Delivery and Response: Closed-circuit television.

Accreditation: Western Association of Schools and Colleges.

For more information, contact: Leslie J. Wright, Associate Dean, Regional and Continuing Education, California State University, Chico, Chico, CA 95929-0250;

Telephone: 916-898-6105; Fax: 916-898-4020; Internet: LWRIGHT@OAVA.CSUCHICO.EDU.

INDIVIDUAL COURSES

California State University, Chico, offers individual for-credit courses in: business/management (undergraduate); computer science (undergraduate and graduate); criminal justice/law (undergraduate); liberal arts/general studies (undergraduate); teacher education (graduate).

PATRICIA SWIFT

Age: 39

Institution: California State University, Chico

Courses taken: Fundamentals of database systems.

Academic goals and achievements: Swift holds an associate degree in computer science from Nashville State Technical Institute. She is working toward her B.S. in computer science.

"I just completed my first distance learning course through a program set up by my employer, AT&T, and I am very impressed with the format. I would like to earn my B.S. degree from California State this way, and I plan to—taking it one class at a time as my job allows.

"There are a number of excellent universities in Nashville, but my main reason for seeking a B.S. through California State's program is that I can easily fit it into my work schedule. The program allows you to make your own class schedule. We receive the tapes two days after the class is held, and I can watch the videotapes either at work—on my lunch hour—or at home.

"I had the telephone number for my instructor, who was *excellent* in her responses to my

questions—not just on the phone but by fax. We'd fax things back and forth: I'd draw diagrams to show her my problem, and she'd draw diagrams and fax them back to give me the answers I needed.

"Since I was just changing jobs within the company and had a heavier workload, I really appreciated that the instructor was able to provide me with extensions on some of my assignments.

"Fundamentals of database systems was a three-credit course with two exams that were monitored by my supervisor. Since the course content was directly related to my job, I received 100 percent tuition reimbursement from AT&T. I look forward to taking more courses this way."

Swift is a system administrator with AT&T.

CALIFORNIA STATE UNIVERSITY, DOMINGUEZ HILLS

CARSON, CA 90747

California State University, Dominguez Hills, first offered a degree program via distance education in 1992.
Total enrollment in distance education programs (1992–93): 100.

The Distance Learning program includes satellite teleconferencing arrangements and delivery of courses to homes, schools, communities, and work sites throughout southern California, using a combination of satellite, cable television, ITFS, and CODEC (compressed and decompressed video).

DEGREE PROGRAMS

PRODUCTION AND INVENTORY CONTROL
Certificate. Consists of five courses designed to provide a broad education in the field.

Requirements: University admission eligibility.

Degree/Certificate Awarded: Postsecondary certificate.

Availability: Open to the public; regional.

Primary Methods of Course Delivery and Response: Cable television.

For more information, contact: Scott Mackay, Director, Training and Development, Extended Education, California State University, Dominguez Hills, 1000 E. Victoria, Carson, CA, 90747; Telephone: 310-516-3355; Fax: 310-516-3971.

PROGRAM FOR ADULT COLLEGE EDUCATION (PACE)
Interdisciplinary liberal arts degree program designed for working adults.

Requirements: 56 lower-division transferable credits.

Degree/Certificate Awarded: Bachelor's—B.A.

Availability: Open to the public; local.

Primary Methods of Course Delivery and Response: Compressed-video television.

For more information, contact: David Heifetz, Director, PACE, Interdisciplinary Studies, California State University, Dominguez Hills, 1000 E. Victoria, Carson, CA, 90747; Telephone: 310-516-3649; Fax: 310-516-3971.

QUALITY ASSURANCE
Master of Science in Quality Assurance. Interdisciplinary program for management personnel responsible for planning and assuring quality of products and services.

Requirements: Bachelor's degree.

Degree/Certificate Awarded: Master's—M.S.

Availability: Open to the public; local.

Primary Methods of Course Delivery and Response: Cable television.

For more information, contact: Scott Mackay, Director, Training and Development, Extended Education, California State University, Dominguez Hills, 1000 E. Victoria, Carson, CA, 90747; Telephone: 310-516-3355; Fax: 310-516-3971.

INDIVIDUAL COURSES

California State University, Dominguez Hills, offers individual for-credit courses in: teacher education (graduate).

CALIFORNIA STATE UNIVERSITY, LOS ANGELES
LOS ANGELES, CA 90032

California State University, Los Angeles, first offered a degree program via distance education in 1987.

Total enrollment in distance education programs (1992–93): 383.

Number graduating from distance programs (spring 1992): 11.

California State University, Los Angeles, students can view courses via ITFS in their workplace, community college, or regional occupational program center. The receive sites are equipped with microwave antennas and two-way audio that allow students to speak with instructors during the broadcast. All receive sites are monitored by a proctor, and students must take examinations under supervision. For education courses, candidates may opt to take basic requirements to clear the Designated Subjects Teaching Credential, selected courses for the Bachelor of Vocational Education (BVE), and selected courses for the master's degree programs in adult and continuing education. Electrical engineering students can take televised courses taught by the authors of the course textbooks.

DEGREE PROGRAM

FIRE PROTECTION ADMINISTRATION AND TECHNOLOGY
Bachelor's degree program that teaches both technical and administrative skills.

Requirements: Same as for on-campus students; must pass a math and writing proficiency exam.

Degree/Certificate Awarded: Bachelor's—B.S.

Availability: Open to the public; Los Angeles basin and surrounding counties.

Primary Methods of Course Delivery and Response: Microwave (ITFS); teleconferencing; videocassette.

On-Campus Component: None.

Accreditation: California State Fire Marshal's Office.

For more information, contact: Chief Ray Shackelford, Advisor, Fire Protection Administration and Technology Program, Department of Technology, California State University, Los Angeles, 5151 State University Drive, Los Angeles, CA 90032; Telephone: 213-343-4550.

INDIVIDUAL COURSES

California State University, Los Angeles, offers individual for-credit courses in: engineering (undergraduate and graduate); fire science (undergraduate); teacher education (undergraduate and graduate).

CALIFORNIA STATE UNIVERSITY, NORTHRIDGE
NORTHRIDGE, CA 91330

California State University, Northridge, first offered a degree program via distance education in 1984.
Total enrollment in distance education programs (1992–93): 150.

DEGREE PROGRAMS

EDUCATION
Teacher Certification for California.

Requirements: Must be a practicing teacher with a bachelor's degree.

Degree/Certificate Awarded: Postsecondary certificate.

Availability: Open to the public; statewide.

Primary Method of Course Delivery and Response: Microwave Instructional Television Service.

For more information, contact: Marlene Perez, Credentials Office, California State University, Northridge, 18111 Nordhoff St., Northridge, CA 91330; Telephone: 818-885-2586.

ENGINEERING
M.S. in Engineering.

Requirements: Same as for on-campus students; 2.5–2.8 GPA.

Degree/Certificate Awarded: Master's—M.S.

Availability: Open to the public; regional. Receive sites include Navy and Edwards Air Force Base.

Primary Method of Course Delivery and Response: Microwave Instructional Television Service.

For more information, contact: Cora Connor, Coordinator, Instructional Television Network, California State University, Northridge, 18111 Nordhoff St., Northridge, CA 91330; 818-885-2355; Fax: 818-885-2316.

INDIVIDUAL COURSES

California State University, Northridge, offers an individual for-credit course in: teacher education (graduate).

CALIFORNIA STATE UNIVERSITY, SACRAMENTO
SACRAMENTO, CA 95825

California State University, Sacramento, first offered a degree program via distance education in 1984.

Total enrollment in distance education programs (1992–93): 10.

Number graduating from distance programs (spring 1992): 1.

California State University, Sacramento, offers an M.B.A. via television (two-way audio, one-way video) to outlying firms and sites.

DEGREE PROGRAMS

BUSINESS ADMINISTRATION
Master's in Business Administration.

Requirements: Bachelor's degree; GMAT; work experience.

Degree/Certificate Awarded: Master's—M.B.A.

Availability: Open to the public; regional.

Primary Methods of Course Delivery and Response: ITFS; teleconferencing.

On-Campus Component: Two to four semester-long classes.

Accreditation: American Assembly of Collegiate Schools of Business.

For more information, contact: Merle Martin, Associate Dean, School of Business Administration, California State University, Sacramento, 6000 J St., Sacramento, CA 95819; Telephone: 916-278-5974; Fax: 916-278-5580.

CHADRON STATE COLLEGE
CHADRON, NE 69337

Chadron State College first offered a degree program via distance education in 1991.

Total enrollment in distance education programs (1992–93): 19.

Number graduating from distance programs (spring 1992): 2.

The Interactive Distance Learning Program at Chadron State College was the first system installed in western Nebraska. Within the next year, the school will have access to a total of nine multipoint connections. The system allows students in rural, isolated communities to participate in courses offered throughout the state. The Interactive Distance Learning Program includes a multimedia production center for enhanced presentations and instruction.

DEGREE PROGRAM

BUSINESS
Master of Business Administration. Program provides exposure to management theory and technical managerial skills as well as to the functional components of business administration.

Requirements: None—open admission institution.

Degree/Certificate Awarded: Master's—M.B.A.

Consortium Affiliation: University of Nebraska in Lincoln.

Availability: Open to the public; regional; service area consists of 25 counties in western and central Nebraska (approximately one third of the state).

Primary Methods of Course Delivery and Response: CD-ROM; compressed-video television; computer conferencing; electronic bulletin board; electronic mail; fax; public television; satellite television; scanner; teleconferencing; telephone; videocassette; videoconferencing; videodisc; videodisc/CD-ROM (multimedia).

For more information, contact: Dr. Roger Wess, Director, Interactive Distance Learning, Department of Education, Chadron State College, 1000 Main St., Chadron, NE 69337; Telephone: 308-432-6364; Fax: 308-432-6464; Internet: IN%"RWESS@CSC1.CSC.EDU".

INDIVIDUAL COURSES

Chadron State College offers individual for-credit courses in: accounting (undergraduate); allied health (undergraduate); business/management (undergraduate and graduate); criminal justice/law (undergraduate); foreign languages (undergraduate); liberal arts/general studies (undergraduate); social work (undergraduate); teacher education (undergraduate and graduate).

COLLEGE OF GREAT FALLS
GREAT FALLS, MT 59405

The College of Great Falls first offered a degree program via distance education in 1980.
Total enrollment in distance education programs (1992–93): 400.

DEGREE PROGRAMS

ACCOUNTING
Interdisciplinary Major-in-Depth in Accounting. Includes financial planning and control, cost behavioral patterns, reporting of financial position and income, auditing, and taxation.

Requirements: Same as for on-campus students.

Degree/Certificate Awarded: Bachelor's—B.S., B.A.

Availability: Open to the public; Montana and Alberta, Canada.

Primary Methods of Course Delivery and Response: Audiocassette; teleconferencing; telephone; videocassette.

For more information, contact: R. K. Bohne, Division Head, Division of Business and Natural Sciences, College of Great Falls, 1301 20th St. South, Great Falls, MT 59405; Telephone: 406-761-8210 ext. 320.

BUSINESS ADMINISTRATION
Major in Business Administration. Academic areas include accounting, economics, finance, business law, management, marketing, and statistics.

Requirements: Same as for on-campus students.

Degree/Certificate Awarded: Bachelor's—B.S., B.A.

Availability: Open to the public; Montana and Alberta, Canada.

Primary Methods of Course Delivery and Response: Audiocassette; teleconferencing; telephone; videocassette.

For more information, contact: R. K. Bohne, Division Head, Division of Business and Natural Sciences, College of Great Falls, 1301 20th St. South, Great Falls, MT 59405; Telephone: 406-761-8210 ext. 320.

COUNSELING PSYCHOLOGY
Understanding of psychology and skills essential to counseling.

Requirements: None.

Degree/Certificate Awarded: Bachelor's—B.A., B.S.

Availability: Open to the public; Montana and Alberta, Canada.

Primary Methods of Course Delivery and Response: Audiocassette; telephone; videocassette.

For more information, contact: Deborah Kottel, J.D., Division Head, Human Services,

College of Great Falls, 1301 20th St. South, Great Falls, MT 59405; Telephone: 406-761-8210; Fax: 406-454-0113.

CRIMINAL JUSTICE
Study of forensic science. Prepares students for careers in law enforcement and the human service side of criminal justice.

Requirements: None.

Degree/Certificate Awarded: Bachelor's—B.A., B.S.

Availability: Open to the public; Montana and Alberta, Canada.

Primary Methods of Course Delivery and Response: Audiocassette; telephone; videocassette.

For more information, contact: Deborah Kottel, J.D., Division Head, Human Services, College of Great Falls, 1301 20th St. South, Great Falls, MT 59405; Telephone: 406-761-8210; Fax: 406-454-0113.

HUMAN SERVICES
Interdisciplinary program with emphasis in psychology, sociology, social work, and other human services fields.

Requirements: None.

Degree/Certificate Awarded: Bachelor's—B.A., B.S.

Availability: Open to the public; Montana and Alberta, Canada.

Primary Methods of Course Delivery and Response: Audiocassette; telephone; videocassette.

For more information, contact: Deborah Kottel, J.D., Division Head, Human Services, College of Great Falls, 1301 20th St. South, Great Falls, MT 59405; Telephone: 406-761-8210; Fax: 406-454-0113.

MICROCOMPUTER MANAGEMENT
Major in Microcomputer Management. Academic areas include information processing, microdata management, microdocument management, MS-DOS, spreadsheets, telecommunications, and software integration.

Requirements: Same as for on-campus students.

Degree/Certificate Awarded: Bachelor's—B.S., B.A.

Availability: Open to the public; Montana and Alberta, Canada.

Primary Methods of Course Delivery and Response: Audiocassette; teleconferencing; telephone; videocassette.

For more information, contact: R. K. Bohne, Division Head, Division of Business and Natural Sciences, College of Great Falls, 1301 20th St. South, Great Falls, MT 59405; Telephone: 406-761-8210 ext. 320.

PARALEGAL STUDIES
Includes pretrial and trial support, tort, criminal law, contract law, and environmental law.

Requirements: None.

Degree/Certificate Awarded: Bachelor's—B.A., B.S.

Availability: Open to the public; Montana and Alberta, Canada.

Primary Methods of Course Delivery and Response: Audiocassette; telephone; videocassette.

For more information, contact: Deborah Kottel, J.D., Division Head, Human Services, College of Great Falls, 1301 20th St. South, Great Falls, MT 59405; Telephone: 406-761-8210; Fax: 406-454-0113.

SOCIOLOGY
Social institutions, community, family, and social and cultural heritage.

Requirements: None.

Degree/Certificate Awarded: Bachelor's—B.A., B.S.

Availability: Open to the public; Montana and Alberta, Canada.

Primary Methods of Course Delivery and Response: Audiocassette; telephone; videocassette.

For more information, contact: Deborah Kottel, J.D., Division Head, Human Services, College of Great Falls, 1301 20th St. South, Great Falls, MT 59405; Telephone: 406-761-8210; Fax: 406-454-0113.

INDIVIDUAL COURSES

The College of Great Falls offers individual for-credit courses in: accounting (undergraduate); allied health (undergraduate); business/management (undergraduate); computer science (undergraduate); criminal justice/law (undergraduate); foreign languages (undergraduate); liberal arts/general studies (undergraduate); social work (undergraduate and graduate); teacher education (undergraduate).

COLORADO STATE UNIVERSITY
FORT COLLINS, CO 80523

Colorado State University first offered a degree program via distance education in 1967.

Total enrollment in distance education programs (1992–93): 2,700.

Number graduating from distance programs (spring 1992): 8.

The Colorado SURGE program delivers graduate education to working professionals who cannot attend regular on-campus classes. An average of 80 courses are taught each semester via SURGE. Regular on-campus courses, taught by Colorado State graduate faculty, are videotaped in specially equipped classrooms. The tapes, along with handouts, are sent via UPS to participating site coordinators. Site coordinators make tapes and materials available to students, provide information about the program, supply registration forms, and proctor exams. SURGE sites are primarily firms that provide on-site coordinators and tuition assistance.

DEGREE PROGRAMS

AGRICULTURAL ENGINEERING
Master's Degree in Agricultural Engineering.

Degree/Certificate Awarded: Master's—M.S.

Availability: Open to the public; national.

Primary Methods of Course Delivery and Response: Computer conferencing; electronic mail; fax; telephone; videocassette.

For more information, contact: Debbie Sheaman, SURGE Coordinator, Division of Continuing Education, Colorado State University, Fort Collins, CO 80523; Telephone: 303-491-5288; Fax: 303-491-7886.

BACHELOR'S DEGREE PROGRAM
Under certain circumstances, students may be eligible to complete a second bachelor's degree via SURGE.

Requirements: Bachelor's degree from an accredited institution; departmental approval.

Degree/Certificate Awarded: Bachelor's—B.A., B.S.

Availability: Open to the public; national.

Primary Methods of Course Delivery and Response: Computer conferencing; electronic mail; fax; telephone; videocassette.

On-Campus Component: Depending on the department, some access to on-campus equipment may be required.

For more information, contact: Debbie Sheaman, SURGE Coordinator, Division of Continuing Education, Colorado State University, Fort Collins, CO 80523; Telephone: 303-491-5288; Fax: 303-491-7886.

BUSINESS ADMINISTRATION
Master's Degree in Business Administration.

Degree/Certificate Awarded: Master's—M.B.A.

Availability: Open to the public; national.

Primary Methods of Course Delivery and Response: Computer conferencing; electronic mail; fax; telephone; videocassette.

For more information, contact: Debbie Sheaman, SURGE Coordinator, Division of Continuing Education, Colorado State University, Fort Collins, CO 80523; Telephone: 303-491-5288; Fax: 303-491-7886.

CHEMICAL ENGINEERING
Master's Degree in Chemical Engineering.

Degree/Certificate Awarded: Master's—M.S.

Availability: Open to the public; national.

Primary Methods of Course Delivery and Response: Computer conferencing; electronic mail; fax; telephone; videocassette.

For more information, contact: Debbie Sheaman, SURGE Coordinator, Division of Continuing Education, Colorado State University, Fort Collins, CO 80523; Telephone: 303-491-5288; Fax: 303-491-7886.

CIVIL ENGINEERING
Master's Degree in Civil Engineering.

Degree/Certificate Awarded: Master's—M.S.

Availability: Open to the public; national.

Primary Methods of Course Delivery and Response: Computer conferencing; electronic mail; fax; telephone; videocassette.

For more information, contact: Debbie Sheaman, SURGE Coordinator, Division of Continuing Education, Colorado State University, Fort Collins, CO 80523; Telephone: 303-491-5288; Fax: 303-491-7886.

COMPUTER SCIENCE
Master's Degree in Computer Science.

Degree/Certificate Awarded: Master's—M.S.

Availability: Open to the public; national.

Primary Methods of Course Delivery and Response: Computer conferencing; electronic mail; fax; telephone; videocassette.

For more information, contact: Debbie Sheaman, SURGE Coordinator, Division of Continuing Education, Colorado State University, Fort Collins, CO 80523; Telephone: 303-491-5288; Fax: 303-491-7886.

ELECTRICAL ENGINEERING
Master's Degree in Electrical Engineering.

Degree/Certificate Awarded: Master's—M.S.

Availability: Open to the public; national.

Primary Methods of Course Delivery and Response: Computer conferencing; electronic mail; fax; telephone; videocassette.

For more information, contact: Debbie Sheaman, SURGE Coordinator, Division of Continuing Education, Colorado State University, Fort Collins, CO 80523; Telephone: 303-491-5288; Fax: 303-491-7886.

INTERDISCIPLINARY ENGINEERING
Master's Degree in Interdisciplinary Engineering. Includes engineering management, environmental engineering, industrial engineering, systems engineering, and optimization.

Degree/Certificate Awarded: Master's—M.S.

Availability: Open to the public; national.

Primary Methods of Course Delivery and Response: Computer conferencing; electronic mail; fax; telephone; videocassette.

For more information, contact: Debbie Sheaman, SURGE Coordinator, Division of Continuing Education, Colorado State University, Fort Collins, CO 80523; Telephone: 303-491-5288; Fax: 303-491-7886.

MANAGEMENT
Master's Degree with Specialization in Management.

Degree/Certificate Awarded: Master's—M.S.

Availability: Open to the public; national.

Primary Methods of Course Delivery and Response: Computer conferencing; electronic mail; fax; telephone; videocassette.

For more information, contact: Debbie Sheaman, SURGE Coordinator, Division of Continuing Education, Colorado State University, Fort Collins, CO 80523; Telephone: 303-491-5288; Fax: 303-491-7886.

MECHANICAL ENGINEERING
Master's Degree in Mechanical Engineering.

Degree/Certificate Awarded: Master's—M.S.

Availability: Open to the public; national.

Primary Methods of Course Delivery and Response: Computer conferencing; electronic mail; fax; telephone; videocassette.

For more information, contact: Debbie Sheaman, SURGE Coordinator, Division of Continuing Education, Colorado State University, Fort Collins, CO 80523; Telephone: 303-491-5288; Fax: 303-491-7886.

Ph.D PROGRAM
Varies with discipline and department.

Requirements: Same as for on-campus Ph.D. candidates.

Degree/Certificate Awarded: Doctorate—Ph.D.

Availability: Open to the public; national.

Primary Methods of Course Delivery and Response: Computer conferencing; electronic mail; fax; telephone; videocassette.

On-Campus Component: Two semesters.

For more information, contact: Debbie Sheaman, SURGE Coordinator, Division of Continuing Education, Colorado State University, Fort Collins, CO 80523; Telephone: 303-491-5288; Fax: 303-491-7886.

STATISTICS
Master's Degree in Statistics.

Degree/Certificate Awarded: Master's—M.S.

Availability: Open to the public; national.

Primary Methods of Course Delivery and Response: Computer conferencing; electronic mail; fax; telephone; videocassette.

For more information, contact: Debbie Sheaman, SURGE Coordinator, Division of Continuing Education, Colorado State University, Fort Collins, CO 80523; Telephone: 303-491-5288; Fax: 303-491-7886.

INDIVIDUAL COURSES

Colorado State University offers individual for-credit courses in: accounting (graduate); business/management (graduate); computer science (graduate); engineering (graduate); liberal arts/general studies (undergraduate); social work (undergraduate); teacher education (graduate).

CORPUS CHRISTI STATE UNIVERSITY
CORPUS CHRISTI, TX 78412

Corpus Christi State University first offered a degree program via distance education in 1983.

Total enrollment in distance education programs (1992–93): 100.

Number graduating from distance programs (spring 1992): 18.

Corpus Christi State University uses the fully interactive, real-time capabilities of the Trans Texas Video Network (TTVN). TTVN is a compressed-video system with two-way audio and visual.

DEGREE PROGRAMS

NURSING
Family Nurse Practitioner Program.

Requirements: Same as for on-campus students.

Degree/Certificate Awarded: Bachelor's—B.S.N., Master's—M.S.N.

Availability: Open to the public; regional.

Primary Method of Course Delivery and Response: Compressed-video television.

On-Campus Component: Varies according to program.

For more information, contact: Christell Bray, Program Director, Family Nurse Practitioner Program, Corpus Christi State University, Corpus Christi, TX 78412; Telephone: 512-994-2463; Fax: 512-993-4204.

INDIVIDUAL COURSES

Corpus Christi State University offers individual for-credit courses in: environmental health and safety (undergraduate); nursing (undergraduate and graduate).

EASTERN OREGON STATE COLLEGE
LA GRANDE, OR 97850

Eastern Oregon State College first offered a degree program via distance education in 1975.
Total enrollment in distance education programs (1992–93): 800.

Number graduating from distance programs (spring 1992): 200.

At Eastern Oregon State College, all distance offerings are built around majors with the intent of permitting students to complete a degree. A full range of student support services is also offered.

DEGREE PROGRAM

EDUCATION
Master's in Teacher Education. Prepares individuals for teacher licensure.

Requirements: GPA; NTE; other factors considered.

Degree/Certificate Awarded: Master's—M.T.E.

Availability: Open to the public; local.

Primary Methods of Course Delivery and Response: Compressed-video television; computer conferencing; satellite television; teleconferencing; telephone.

On-Campus Component: Summer session.

Accreditation: National Council for Accredication of Teacher Education.

For more information, contact: Jens Robinson, Dean, School of Education, Eastern Oregon State College, La Grande, OR 97850; Telephone: 503-962-3772.

INDIVIDUAL COURSES

Eastern Oregon State College offers individual for-credit courses in: business/management (undergraduate); teacher education (graduate).

EMBRY-RIDDLE AERONAUTICAL UNIVERSITY
DAYTONA BEACH, FL 32114-3900

Embry-Riddle Aeronautical University first offered a degree program via distance education in 1982.

Total enrollment in distance education programs (1992–93): 2,500.

Number graduating from distance programs (spring 1992): 21.

At Embry-Riddle Aeronautical University, undergraduate terms are 15 weeks long and begin every Friday. Courses are via audiotape or videotape, and some use an electronic bulletin board system.

DEGREE PROGRAMS

AERONAUTICS

Bachelor of Science in Professional Aeronautics—126 semester hours.

Requirements: High school diploma or GED; aviation background.

Degree/Certificate Awarded: Bachelor's—B.S.P.A.

Availability: Open to aviation specialties; worldwide.

Primary Method of Course Delivery and Response: Audiocassette.

For more information, contact: Thomas W. Pettit, Director, Department of Independent Studies, Embry-Riddle Aeronautical University, 600 S. Clyde Morris Blvd., Daytona Beach, FL 32114; Telephone: 904-226-6397; Fax: 904-226-6949.

AERONAUTICS

Master of Aeronautical Science. A 36-semester-hour program, including a graduate research project.

Requirements: B.S.; 2.5 GPA; GRE score of 1,000 on verbal and quantitative sections.

Degree/Certificate Awarded: Master's—M.A.S.

Availability: Open to the public; worldwide.

Primary Methods of Course Delivery and Response: Electronic bulletin board; videocassette.

For more information, contact: James Gallogly, Manager, Graduate Program, Department of Independent Studies, Embry-Riddle Aeronautical University, 600 S. Clyde Morris Blvd., Daytona Beach, FL 32114; Telephone: 800-866-6271; Fax: 904-226-6949.

AVIATION

Aviation Business Administration. A 126-semester-hour program.

Requirements: High school diploma or GED.

Degree/Certificate Awarded: Bachelor's—B.S.

Availability: Open to the public; worldwide.

Primary Method of Course Delivery and Response: Audiocassette.

For more information, contact: Thomas W. Pettit, Director, Department of Independent Studies, Embry-Riddle Aeronautical University, 600 S. Clyde Morris Blvd., Daytona Beach, FL 32114; Telephone: 904-226-6397; Fax: 904-226-6949.

INDIVIDUAL COURSES

Embry-Riddle Aeronautical University offers individual for-credit courses in: accounting (undergraduate); aviation business/management (undergraduate); computer science (undergraduate); criminal justice/law (undergraduate); liberal arts/general studies (undergraduate).

FLORIDA ATLANTIC UNIVERSITY
BOCA RATON, FL 33431

Florida Atlantic University first offered a degree program via distance education in 1991.

DEGREE PROGRAMS

CIVIL ENGINEERING
Degree/Certificate Awarded: Master's—M.S., M.E.

Availability: Open to the public; statewide.

Primary Methods of Course Delivery and Response: Closed-circuit television; ITFS 4-channel; telephone; videocassette.

On-Campus Component: Varies.

For more information, contact: W. Douglas Trabert, Director of Instructional Services, Florida Atlantic University, 500 NW 20th St., Boca Raton, FL 33431; Telephone: 407-367-2373; Fax: 407-338-3863; Internet: TRABERT@ACC.FAU.EDU; Bitnet: TRABERT@FAUVAX.

COMPUTER SCIENCE AND ENGINEERING
Degree/Certificate Awarded: Master's—M.S., M.E.

Availability: Open to the public; statewide.

Primary Methods of Course Delivery and Response: Closed-circuit television; ITFS 4-channel; telephone; videocassette.

On-Campus Component: Varies.

For more information, contact: W. Douglas Trabert, Director of Instructional Services, Florida Atlantic University, 500 NW 20th St., Boca Raton, FL 33431; Telephone: 407-367-2373; Fax: 407-338-3863; Internet: TRABERT@ACC.FAU.EDU; Bitnet: TRABERT@FAUVAX.

ELECTRICAL ENGINEERING
Degree/Certificate Awarded: Master's—M.S., M.E.

Availability: Open to the public; statewide.

Primary Methods of Course Delivery and Response: Closed-circuit television; ITFS 4-channel; telephone; videocassette.

On-Campus Component: Varies.

For more information, contact: W. Douglas Trabert, Director of Instructional Services, Florida Atlantic University, 500 NW 20th St., Boca Raton, FL 33431; Telephone: 407-367-2373; Fax: 407-338-3863; Internet: TRABERT@ACC.FAU.EDU; Bitnet: TRABERT@FAUVAX.

MANUFACTURING SYSTEMS ENGINEERING
Degree/Certificate Awarded: Master's—M.S., M.E.

Availability: Open to the public; statewide.

Primary Methods of Course Delivery and Response: Closed-circuit television; ITFS 4-channel; telephone; videocassette.

On-Campus Component: Varies.

For more information, contact: W. Douglas Trabert, Director of Instructional Services, Florida Atlantic University, 500 NW 20th St., Boca Raton, FL 33431; Telephone: 407-367-2373; Fax: 407-338-3863; Internet: TRABERT@ACC.FAU.EDU; Bitnet: TRABERT@FAUVAX.

MECHANICAL ENGINEERING
Degree/Certificate Awarded: Master's—M.S., M.E.

Availability: Open to the public; statewide.

Primary Methods of Course Delivery and Response: Closed-circuit television; ITFS 4-channel; telephone; videocassette.

On-Campus Component: Varies.

For more information, contact: W. Douglas Trabert, Director of Instructional Services, Florida Atlantic University, 500 NW 20th St., Boca Raton, FL 33431; Telephone: 407-367-2373; Fax: 407-338-3863; Internet: TRABERT@ACC.FAU.EDU; Bitnet: TRABERT@FAUVAX.

OCEAN ENGINEERING
Degree/Certificate Awarded: Master's—M.S., M.E.

Availability: Open to the public; statewide.

Primary Methods of Course Delivery and Response: Closed-circuit television; ITFS 4-channel; telephone; videocassette.

On-Campus Component: Varies.

For more information, contact: W. Douglas Trabert, Director of Instructional Services, Florida Atlantic University, 500 NW 20th St., Boca Raton, FL 33431; Telephone: 407-367-2373; Fax: 407-338-3863; Internet: TRABERT@ACC.FAU.EDU; Bitnet: TRABERT@FAUVAX.

INDIVIDUAL COURSES
Florida Atlantic University offers individual for-credit courses in: business/management (graduate); engineering (graduate); teacher education (graduate).

FLORIDA STATE UNIVERSITY
TALLAHASSEE, FL 32306

Florida State University first offered a degree program via distance education in 1990.

Total enrollment in distance education programs (1992–93): 35.

Number graduating from distance programs (spring 1992): 17.

DEGREE PROGRAMS

ELECTRICAL ENGINEERING
Specialties in computer engineering, digital signal processing and controls.

Requirements: Bachelor's degree in electrical engineering; 3.0 GPA last two years; 1000 on GRE.

Degree/Certificate Awarded: Master's—M.S.

Consortium Affiliation: FAMU/FASU, Tallahassee, FL.

Availability: Open to the public; local.

Primary Method of Course Delivery and Response: Compressed-video television.

On-Campus Component: Offered electronically to the Panama City Campus.

For more information, contact: Dr. William Jerome Barnes, Associate Dean, Florida State University Panama City Campus, 4750 Collegiate Drive, Panama City, Florida 32405; Telephone: 904-872-4750; Fax: 904-872-4199.

MECHANICAL ENGINEERING
Specialties in fluid mechanics and heat transfer, solid mechanics and materials, dynamics and controls.

Requirements: Bachelor's degree in mechanical engineering; 3.0 GPA last two years; 1000 cumulative GRE score.

Degree/Certificate Awarded: Master's—M.S.M.E.

Consortium Affiliation: FAMU/FSU, Tallahassee, FL.

Availability: Open to the public; local.

Primary Method of Course Delivery and Response: Compressed-video television.

On-Campus Component: Offered electronically to the Panama City Campus.

For more information, contact: Dr. William Jerome Barnes, Associate Dean, Florida State University Panama City Campus, 4750 Collegiate Drive, Panama City, Florida 32405; Telephone: 904-872-4750; Fax: 904-872-4199.

GEORGE WASHINGTON UNIVERSITY
WASHINGTON, DC 20052

George Washington University first offered a degree program via distance education in 1983.
Total enrollment in distance education programs (1992–93): 332.

At George Washington University, programs are composed of a combination of technologies. Distribution is national, including cable systems, satellite broadcasts, open circuit broadcasting, compressed video, and tape shipment.

DEGREE PROGRAMS

EDUCATIONAL TECHNOLOGY
Educational Technology Leadership Master's Degree Program.

Requirements: None for individual courses; GRE or MAT for admission to M.A. program.

Degree/Certificate Awarded: Master's—M.A.

Availability: Open to the public; national.

Primary Methods of Course Delivery and Response: Cable television; computer conferencing; electronic bulletin board; electronic mail; satellite television; teleconferencing; telephone.

For more information, contact: Dr. William Lynch, Professor, Educational Technology Leadership, 2201 G Street, Washington, DC 20052; Telephone: 202-994-6862; Fax: 202-994-5870; Bitnet: BLYNCH@GWUVM.

ELECTRICAL ENGINEERING/COMPUTER SCIENCE
Individual courses in communication systems and computer networking.

Requirements: Admission to the graduate program at National Technological University.

Degree/Certificate Awarded: Master's—M.S.

Consortium Affiliation: National Technological University.

Availability: Open to the public; national.

Primary Methods of Course Delivery and Response: Compressed-video television; satellite television; teleconferencing; videocassette.

For more information, contact: Thomas M. Wing, Station Manager, GW Television, George Washington University, Academic Center T306, Washington, DC 20052; Telephone: 202-994-8233; Fax: 202-994-5048; Bitnet: TOMWING@GWUVM.

QUALITY MANAGEMENT
Quality Management Series. One-day satellite seminars presented live by leading quality management experts.

Requirements: None.

Degree/Certificate Awarded: Postsecondary certificate.

Availability: Open to the public; national.

Primary Methods of Course Delivery and Response: Satellite television; teleconferencing; telephone; videocassette; videoconferencing.

For more information, contact: Mary Lou Bishop, Director, George Washington National Satellite Network, Continuing Engineering Education, Academic Center T308, George Washington University, Washington, DC 20052; Telephone: 202-676-5117; Fax: 202-785-3382.

INDIVIDUAL COURSES

George Washington University offers individual for-credit courses in: business/management (graduate); computer science (graduate); engineering (graduate); teacher education (graduate).

GEORGIA INSTITUTE OF TECHNOLOGY
ATLANTA, GA 30332

Georgia Institute of Technology first offered a degree program via distance
education in 1975.

Total enrollment in distance education programs (1992–93): 300.

Number graduating from distance programs (spring 1992): 7.

*Georgia Tech's video-based instruction system (VBIS) delivers graduate-level courses
in six fields of engineering nationwide. Video cameras record instructor presentations
and student-instructor interactions during regular Georgia Tech graduate classes.
Videotape and supporting materials are sent to off-campus students, who participate
in classroom activities by watching the taped classes on video monitors at their
workplace or at home. Students admitted to Georgia Tech for graduate study through
the video program are assigned an academic adviser. Students communicate with
their adviser and the course instructors by telephone, fax, or electronic mail.*

DEGREE PROGRAMS

ELECTRICAL ENGINEERING
Areas include computer engineering, digital signal processing, electric power, and
telecommunications.

Degree/Certificate Awarded: Master's—M.S.

Availability: Open to the public; national.

Primary Method of Course Delivery and Response: Videocassette.

Accreditation: Southern Association of Colleges and Schools, Accreditation Board
for Engineering and Technology.

For more information, contact: Joseph S. Boland, Associate Director, Continuing
Education, Georgia Institute of Technology, Atlanta, GA 30332-0240; Telephone:
404-894-8572; Fax: 404-894-8924; Internet:joseph_boland@conted.gatech.edu;
Bitnet: joseph_boland@conted.gatech.edu.

ENGINEERING
Computer Integrated Manufacturing Systems. Designated to strike a balance
between technical depth and broad comprehension of the challenges facing
industry.

Degree/Certificate Awarded: Postsecondary certificate.

Availability: Open to the public; national.

Primary Method of Course Delivery and Response: Videocassette.

Accreditation: Southern Association of Colleges and Schools, Accredition Board for
Engineering and Technology.

For more information, contact: Joseph S. Boland, Associate Director, Continuing
Education, Georgia Institute of Technology, Atlanta, GA 30332-0240; Telephone:

404-894-8572; Fax: 404-894-8924; Internet:joseph_boland@conted.gatech.edu; Bitnet: joseph_boland@conted.gatech.edu.

ENGINEERING

Test and Evaluation.

Degree/Certificate Awarded: Postsecondary certificate.

Availability: Open to the public; national.

Primary Method of Course Delivery and Response: Videocassette.

Accreditation: Southern Association of Colleges and Schools, Accreditation Board for Engineering and Technology.

For more information, contact: Joseph S. Boland, Associate Director, Continuing Education, Georgia Institute of Technology, Atlanta, GA 30332-0240; Telephone: 404-894-8572; Fax: 404-894-8924; Internet:joseph_boland@conted.gatech.edu; Bitnet: joseph_boland@conted.gatech.edu.

ENVIRONMENTAL ENGINEERING

May include courses in water quality and treatment, wastewater reclamation and disposal, solid- and hazardous-waste management, groundwater management, and water resources management.

Degree/Certificate Awarded: Master's—M.S.

Availability: Open to the public; national.

Primary Method of Course Delivery and Response: Videocassette.

Accreditation: Southern Association of Colleges and Schools, Accreditation Board for Engineering and Technology.

For more information, contact: Joseph S. Boland, Associate Director, Continuing Education, Georgia Institute of Technology, Atlanta, GA 30332-0240; Telephone: 404-894-8572; Fax: 404-894-8924; Internet:joseph_boland@conted.gatech.edu; Bitnet: joseph_boland@conted.gatech.edu.

HEALTH PHYSICS

An applied science concerned with the protection of people and the environment from the hazards of radiation and chemical pollutants.

Degree/Certificate Awarded: Master's—M.S.

Availability: Open to the public; national.

Primary Method of Course Delivery and Response: Videocassette.

Accreditation: Southern Association of Colleges and Schools, Accreditation Board for Engineering and Technology.

For more information, contact: Joseph S. Boland, Associate Director, Continuing Education, Georgia Institute of Technology, Atlanta, GA 30332-0240; Telephone: 404-894-8572; Fax: 404-894-8924; Internet:joseph_boland@conted.gatech.edu; Bitnet: joseph_boland@conted.gatech.edu.

INDUSTRIAL ENGINEERING

Fundamental themes include automation, production and logistics systems, and statistical process control and quality assurance.

Degree/Certificate Awarded: Master's—M.S.

Availability: Open to the public; national.

Primary Method of Course Delivery and Response: Videocassette.

Accreditation: Southern Association of Colleges and Schools, Accreditation Board for Engineering and Technology.

For more information, contact: Joseph S. Boland, Associate Director, Continuing Education, Georgia Institute of Technology, Atlanta, GA 30332-0240; Telephone: 404-894-8572; Fax: 404-894-8924; Internet:joseph_boland@conted.gatech.edu; Bitnet: joseph_boland@conted.gatech.edu.

MECHANICAL ENGINEERING

Concentrations in thermal science and mechanical systems.

Degree/Certificate Awarded: Master's—M.S.

Availability: Open to the public; national.

Primary Method of Course Delivery and Response: Videocassette.

Accreditation: Southern Association of Colleges and Schools, Accreditation Board for Engineering and Technology.

For more information, contact: Joseph S. Boland, Associate Director, Continuing Education, Georgia Institute of Technology, Atlanta, GA 30332-0240; Telephone: 404-894-8572; Fax: 404-894-8924; Internet:joseph_boland@conted.gatech.edu; Bitnet: joseph_boland@conted.gatech.edu.

NUCLEAR ENGINEERING

Concerned with the release, control, utilization, and environmental impact of energy from nuclear fission and fusion sources.

Degree/Certificate Awarded: Master's—M.S.

Availability: Open to the public; national.

Primary Method of Course Delivery and Response: Videocassette.

Accreditation: Southern Association of Colleges and Schools, Accreditation Board for Engineering and Technology.

For more information, contact: Joseph S. Boland, Associate Director, Continuing Education, Georgia Institute of Technology, Atlanta, GA 30332-0240; Telephone: 404-894-8572; Fax: 404-894-8924; Internet:joseph_boland@conted.gatech.edu; Bitnet: joseph_boland@conted.gatech.edu.

INDIVIDUAL COURSES

Georgia Institute of Technology offers an individual for-credit course in: engineering (graduate).

GOVERNORS STATE UNIVERSITY

UNIVERSITY PARK, IL 60466

Governors State University first offered a degree program via distance education in 1973.

Total enrollment in distance education programs (1992–93): 1,993.

Number graduating from distance programs (spring 1992): 77.

The Board of Governors Bachelor's Degree Program at Governors State University offers a liberal arts degree to adult learners, characterized by extensive use of prior learning assessment and media-based courses.

DEGREE PROGRAM

LIBERAL ARTS

Board of Governors Bachelor's Degree Program.

Requirements: 60 credit hours with minimum 2.0 GPA.

Degree/Certificate Awarded: Bachelor's—B.A.

Consortium Affiliation: Board of Governors Universities, Springfield, IL.

Availability: Open to the public; national.

Primary Methods of Course Delivery and Response: Cable television; computer diskette; fax; teleconferencing; telephone; videoconferencing.

Accreditation: Council for Adult and Experiential Learning.

For more information, contact: Dr. Otis O. Lawrence, Director, BOG/B.A. Degree Program, CELCS, Governors State University, University Park, IL, 60466; Telephone: 708-534-7279; Fax: 708-534-8458.

INDIVIDUAL COURSES

Governors State University offers individual for-credit courses in: accounting (undergraduate); allied health (undergraduate and graduate); business/management (undergraduate); liberal arts/general studies (undergraduate and graduate); teacher education (undergraduate and graduate).

GRAND VALLEY STATE UNIVERSITY
ALLENDALE, MI 49401

Grand Valley State University first offered a degree program via distance education in 1989.

Total enrollment in distance education programs (1992–93): 444.

Number graduating from distance programs (spring 1992): 73.

Grand Valley State University offers live, interactive courses via satellite television. A degree completion program in nursing (for RNs/ADNs) and graduate-level endorsement programs in education are offered. The nursing program is delivered to six distant sites in Michigan: Alma, Benton Harbor, Harrison, Muskegon, Scottville, and Sidney. The education program is delivered to over 20 sites, from Michigan's Upper Peninsula to the Indiana border.

DEGREE PROGRAMS

EARLY CHILDHOOD/PRE-PRIMARY IMPAIRED ENDORSEMENT
All courses necessary for certified teachers to add endorsements to their certificate.

Requirements: Certified teacher; undergraduate GPA considered.

Degree/Certificate Awarded: Postsecondary certificate.

Availability: Open to the public; statewide.

Primary Methods of Course Delivery and Response: Satellite television.

For more information, contact: Terry Gorsky, Assistant, Grandlink Satellite Programs, Grand Valley State University, 301 West Fulton St., Grand Rapids, WI 49504; Telephone: 616-771-6618; Fax: 616-771-6520.

NURSING
Bachelor of Science in Nursing Degree Completion Program. All courses necessary to complete the B.S.N. degree.

Requirements: RN or ADN; current license; previous GPA considered.

Degree/Certificate Awarded: Bachelor's—B.S.N.

Availability: Open to the public; statewide.

Primary Method of Course Delivery and Response: Satellite television.

For more information, contact: Terry Gorsky, Assistant, Grandlink Satellite Programs, Grand Valley State University, 301 West Fulton St., Grand Rapids, WI 49504; Telephone: 616-771-6618; Fax: 616-771-6520.

INDIVIDUAL COURSES

Grand Valley State University offers an individual for-credit course in: teacher education (graduate).

INDIANA STATE UNIVERSITY
TERRE HAUTE, IN 47809

Indiana State University first offered a degree program via distance education in 1989.

Total enrollment in distance education programs (1992–93): 150.

Number graduating from distance programs (spring 1992): 14.

Indiana State University offers distance learning via interactive television—one-way video and two-way audio—through the state-operated Indiana Higher Education Telecommunications System. Videotapes of classes are available to students when needed.

DEGREE PROGRAMS

HUMAN RESOURCE DEVELOPMENT FOR HIGHER EDUCATION AND INDUSTRY
Master's degree program. Focuses on planning, managing, organizing, and evaluating education, training, and other human resource development activities.

Requirements: Bachelor's degree; 2.5 GPA; other requirements vary.

Degree/Certificate Awarded: Master's—M.S.

Availability: Open to the public; statewide.

Primary Method of Course Delivery and Response: Closed-circuit television.

For more information, contact: Lowell Anderson, Chair, Industrial Technology Education Department, Indiana State University, Terre Haute, IN 47809; Telephone: 812-237-2642.

OCCUPATIONAL SAFETY MANAGEMENT
Features courses in systems safety, human factors engineering, program management and evaluation, safety law, and policy analysis.

Requirements: Bachelor's degree; one year of college chemistry and mathematics; other requirements or options vary.

Degree/Certificate Awarded: Master's—M.S.

Availability: Open to the public; statewide.

Primary Method of Course Delivery and Response: Closed-circuit television.

For more information, contact: Portia Plummer, Chairperson, Health and Safety, Indiana State University, Terre Haute, IN 47809; Telephone: 812-237-3071.

INDIVIDUAL COURSES

Indiana State University offers individual for-credit courses in: accounting (undergraduate); business/management (undergraduate); environmental health and safety (graduate); human resource development (undergraduate and graduate); industrial technical education (undergraduate and graduate); teacher education (graduate).

IOWA STATE UNIVERSITY OF SCIENCE AND TECHNOLOGY
AMES, IA 50011

Iowa State University of Science and Technology first offered a degree program via distance education in 1965.
Total enrollment in distance education programs (1992–93): 1,000.

Number graduating from distance programs (spring 1992): 20.

Iowa State University of Science and Technology offers an academically rigorous program of master's level and upper-level undergraduate course work.

DEGREE PROGRAMS

AGRICULTURE
Professional Agriculture Bachelor of Science Degree. Junior and senior course work for undergraduate degree, focusing on animal science, plant and soil science, and agricultural social science and economics.

Requirements: High school diploma; progress toward 64 college credits.

Degree/Certificate Awarded: Bachelor's—B.S.

Availability: Open to the public; regional.

Primary Methods of Course Delivery and Response: Compressed-video television; Iowa Communications Network (fiber optics); satellite television; videocassette.

On-Campus Component: One week during one summer. Many courses require one Saturday on campus per credit.

For more information, contact: Mark Honeyman, Coordinator of Professional Agriculture, College of Agriculture, Iowa State University of Science and Technology, 20 Curtiss Hall, Ames, IA 50011; Telephone: 515-294-9666, 800-747-4478; Fax: 515-294-5334.

AGRICULTURE
Master of Agriculture. Professional master's degree for farmers and those in agribusiness, focusing on animal science, horticulture, economics, agronomy, and agricultural technical systems.

Requirements: Bachelor's degree from an accredited institution.

Degree/Certificate Awarded: Master's—M.Ag.

Availability: Open to the public; regional.

Primary Methods of Course Delivery and Response: Compressed-video television; Iowa Communications Network (fiber optics); satellite television; videocassette.

On-Campus Component: One week during one summer. Many courses require one Saturday on campus per credit.

For more information, contact: Mark Honeyman, Coordinator of Professional

Agriculture, College of Agriculture, Iowa State University of Science and Technology, 20 Curtiss Hall, Ames, IA 50011; Telephone: 515-294-9666, 800-747-4478; Fax: 515-294-5334.

ENGINEERING

Master's Degree in Engineering. Advanced undergraduate and graduate courses in aerospace, agriculture and biosystems, chemical, civil, computer, electrical, industrial, mechanical, and nuclear engineering delivered to business and industry sites.

Requirements: Bachelor's degree from an accredited school.

Degree/Certificate Awarded: Master's—M.S., M.E.

Availability: Open to the public; national.

Primary Methods of Course Delivery and Response: Electronic mail; fax; Iowa Communications Network (fiber optics); telephone; videocassette.

For more information, contact: Edwin C. Jones, Coordinator, Professional Programs Office, Iowa State University of Science and Technology, 240 Engineering Annex, Ames, IA 50011; Telephone: 515-294-4962; Fax: 515-294-6184; Internet: n2.ecg@isu mvs.iastate. edu.

INDIVIDUAL COURSES

Iowa State University of Science and Technology offers individual for-credit courses in: agriculture (undergraduate and graduate); engineering (undergraduate and graduate); liberal arts/general studies (undergraduate); teacher education (graduate).

KANSAS NEWMAN COLLEGE
WICHITA, KS 67213

Kansas Newman College first offered a degree program via distance education in 1988.

Total enrollment in distance education programs (1992–93): 50.

Number graduating from distance programs (spring 1992): 9.

Kansas Newman College offers a complete program for RNs in rural Kansas, designed to produce a generalist in nursing and to provide a basis for advanced education in nursing.

DEGREE PROGRAM

NURSING

Off-Campus Bachelor of Science in Nursing Program. Curriculum combines liberal arts and science courses to provide a general and professional education for RNs.

Requirements: 2.0 GPA; interview with B.S.N. faculty; evidence of professional liability; health exam.

Degree/Certificate Awarded: Bachelor's—B.S.N.

Availability: Open to RNs; statewide.

Primary Method of Course Delivery and Response: Videocassette.

Accreditation: National League for Nursing, North Central, Kansas Department of Education.

For more information, contact: Sr. Glenda Reimer, Director of Off-Campus Nursing, Nursing Division, Kansas Newman College, 3100 McCormick, Wichita, KS 67213; Telephone: 316-942-4291; Fax: 316-942-4483.

INDIVIDUAL COURSES

Kansas Newman College offers an individual for-credit course in: nursing (undergraduate).

KANSAS STATE UNIVERSITY
MANHATTAN, KS 66506

Total enrollment in distance education programs (1992–93): 350.
Number graduating from distance programs (spring 1992): 20.

DEGREE PROGRAMS

AGRICULTURE AND ANIMAL SCIENCES AND INDUSTRY
Non-Traditional Studies. Bachelor's degree program.

Requirements: Minimum of 60 college credits; 2.0 GPA.

Degree/Certificate Awarded: Bachelor's—B.S.

Consortium Affiliation: National University Degree Consortium of Mind Extension University, Colorado.

Availability: Open to the public; national.

Primary Methods of Course Delivery and Response: Audiocassette; cable television; teleconferencing; videocassette.

On-Campus Component: One week.

For more information, contact: Cyndy Trent, Non-Traditional Studies Coordinator, Division of Continuing Education, Academic Outreach, Kansas State University, 218 College Court Building, Manhattan, KS 66506; Telephone: 800-622-2KSU; Fax: 913-532-5637.

FOOD SCIENCE
Food Science Certificate. Provides in-depth knowledge for managers, supervisors, and food technologists to improve the quality of food products, meet stringent federal inspection standards, and increase efficiency of operations.

Requirements: None.

Degree/Certificate Awarded: Postsecondary certificate.

Availability: Open to the public; national and international.

Primary Methods of Course Delivery and Response: Audiocassette; teleconferencing; videocassette.

On-Campus Component: One week.

Accreditation: USDA/Food Safety and Inspection Service.

For more information, contact: Linda Henderson, Division of Continuing Education, Distance Learning Program, Kansas State University, 226 College Court Building, Manhattan, KS 66506; Telephone: 913-532-5686; Fax: 913-532-5637; Internet: HENDERS@KSUM.KSU.EDU.

SOCIAL SCIENCES
Non-Traditional Studies. Interdisciplinary bachelor of science degree program. Only available to bachelor's degree students.

Requirements: Minimum of 60 college credits; 2.0 GPA.

Degree/Certificate Awarded: Bachelor's—B.S.

Consortium Affiliation: National University Degree Consortium, Mind Extension University, Colorado.

Availability: Open to the public; national.

Primary Methods of Course Delivery and Response: Audiocassette; cable television; teleconferencing; telephone; videocassette.

For more information, contact: Cyndy Trent, Non-Traditional Studies Coordinator, Division of Continuing Education, Academic Outreach, Kansas State University, 218 College Court Building, Manhattan, KS 66506; Telephone: 800-622-2KSU; Fax: 913-532-5637.

INDIVIDUAL COURSES
Kansas State University offers individual for-credit courses in: agriculture (undergraduate and graduate); business/management (undergraduate and graduate); liberal arts/general studies (undergraduate and graduate).

LEHIGH UNIVERSITY
BETHLEHEM, PA 18015

Lehigh University first offered a degree program via distance education in 1992. Total enrollment in distance education programs (1992–93): 100.

Lehigh University broadcasts regular on-campus courses live via satellite to distance education students. Students interact with their class by calling an 800 number and having their call broadcast to the class. Lehigh University is also implementing an interactive computer-based audiographics system that allows distance education students and professors to write on an interactive "blackboard."

DEGREE PROGRAMS

CHEMISTRY
Master's Degree in Chemistry. A 30-credit-hour degree with a 6-credit-hour research component.

Requirements: Bachelor's degree.

Degree/Certificate Awarded: Master's—M.S.

Availability: Open to a restricted group—must be company-sponsored; national.

Primary Method of Course Delivery and Response: Satellite television.

For more information, contact: Peg Kercsmar, Program Administrator, Distance Education, Lehigh University, 205 Johnson Hall, Bethlehem, PA 18015; Telephone: 215-758-5794; Fax: 215-974-6427; Internet: MAKS@LEH.

CHEMICAL ENGINEERING
Master's Degree in Chemical Engineering. A 30-credit-hour degree; no research component.

Requirements: Bachelor's degree.

Degree/Certificate Awarded: Master's—M.S.

Availability: Open to a restricted group—must be company-sponsored; national.

Primary Method of Course Delivery and Response: Satellite television.

For more information, contact: Peg Kercsmar, Program Administrator, Distance Education, Lehigh University, 205 Johnson Hall, Bethlehem, PA 18015; Telephone: 215-758-5794; Fax: 215-974-6427; Internet: MAKS@LEH.

INDIVIDUAL COURSES

Lehigh University offers individual for-credit courses in: engineering (graduate); environmental health and safety (graduate); teacher education (graduate).

LOYOLA UNIVERSITY, NEW ORLEANS
NEW ORLEANS, LA 70118

Loyola University, New Orleans, first offered a degree program via distance education in 1991.
Total enrollment in distance education programs (1992–93): 174.

Loyola University's Off-Campus Learning Program delivers videotaped courses leading to the B.S.N. degree to nurses at distant sites throughout Louisiana. The school will add other degree programs in the future.

DEGREE PROGRAM

<u>NURSING</u>
Off-Campus Learning Program. Offers courses to RNs in Loyola University's RN to B.S.N. program.

Requirements: RN license.

Degree/Certificate Awarded: Bachelor's—B.S.N..

Availability: Open to RNs.

Primary Method of Course Delivery and Response: Videocassette.

On-Campus Component: Varies by course. One-day orientation and one day for first nursing course are mandatory.

Accreditation: Southern Association of Colleges and Schools (pending); National League for Nursing (pending).

For more information, contact: Nancy McKenzie, Coordinator, Off-Campus Learning Program, Loyola University, New Orleans, Box 14, 6363 St. Charles Avenue, New Orleans, LA 70118; 800-488-OCLP; Fax: 504-865-3883.

INDIVIDUAL COURSES

Loyola University, New Orleans, offers an individual for-credit course in: nursing (undergraduate).

MARY WASHINGTON COLLEGE
FREDERICKSBURG, VA 22401

Mary Washington College first offered a degree program via distance education in 1987.

Total enrollment in distance education programs (1992–93): 108.

Number graduating from distance programs (spring 1992): 2.

Graduate classes delivered live, via satellite, in engineering (degrees offered from Virginia Tech, University of Virginia, and Old Dominion University) and business administration (Virginia Tech degree).

DEGREE PROGRAMS

BUSINESS ADMINISTRATION
Master of Business Administration.

Requirements: GMAT; four-year accredited undergraduate degree.

Degree/Certificate Awarded: Master's—M.B.A.

Availability: Open to the public; statewide.

Primary Methods of Course Delivery and Response: Satellite television; telephone.

Accreditation: American Association of Collegiate Schools of Business.

For more information, contact: Alan Brown, Coordinator of Distance Learning, Center for Graduate and Continuing Education, Mary Washington College, 1301 College Ave., Fredericksburg, VA 22401; Telephone: 703-899-4628; Fax: 703-899-4373.

ENGINEERING
Commonwealth Graduate Engineering Program. Graduate engineering degrees in electrical, mechanical, nuclear, aerospace and ocean, systems, civil, chemical, and administration and management.

Requirements: Four-year accredited undergraduate degree; GRE (for some programs); references.

Degree/Certificate Awarded: Master's—M.E.

Consortium Affiliation: Virginia Cooperative Graduate Engineering Program, 211 Hibbs Bldg., Suite 211, 900 Park Ave., Richmond, VA 23284.

Availability: Open to the public; international.

Primary Methods of Course Delivery and Response: Satellite television, telephone.

For more information, contact: Alan Brown, Coordinator of Distance Learning, Center for Graduate and Continuing Education, Mary Washington College, 1301 College Ave., Fredericksburg, VA 22401; Telephone: 703-899-4628; Fax: 703-899-4373.

MOUNT SAINT VINCENT UNIVERSITY
HALIFAX, NOVA SCOTIA B3M 2J6, CANADA

Mount Saint Vincent University first offered a degree program via distance education in 1982.
Total enrollment in distance education programs (1992–93): 350.

DEGREE PROGRAMS

BUSINESS ADMINISTRATION
Certificate in Business Administration. Provides students with a basic introduction to the field.

Degree/Certificate Awarded: Postsecondary certificate.

Availability: Open to the public; national (Canada).

Primary Methods of Course Delivery and Response: Teleconferencing; telephone; videocassette.

For more information, contact: Carolyn Nobes, Open Learning Coordinator, Tourism and Hospitality Management, Mount Saint Vincent University, EMF Rm. 121, 166 Bedford Hwy., Halifax, Nova Scotia B3M 2J6, Canada; Telephone: 902-457-6511; Fax: 902-457-2618.

GERONTOLOGY
Gerontology Certificate.

Degree/Certificate Awarded: Postsecondary certificate.

Availability: Open to the public; Atlantic Canada.

Primary Methods of Course Delivery and Response: Satellite television; teleconferencing; videoconferencing.

For more information, contact: Wendy McLean, Secretary, DUET, Mount Saint Vincent University, 166 Bedford Hwy., Halifax, Nova Scotia B3M 2J6, Canada; Telephone: 902-457-6437; Fax: 902-457-2618.

TOURISM AND HOSPITALITY
Tourism and Hospitality Management Degree. Integrates theories of food, beverage, and accommodation management with tourism development and planning to give graduates an understanding of the industry.

Requirements: Grade 12 completion with 65 percent average.

Degree/Certificate Awarded: Bachelor's—B.T.H.M.

Availability: Open to the public; national (Canada).

Primary Methods of Course Delivery and Response: Teleconferencing; telephone; videocassette.

For more information, contact: Carolyn Nobes, Open Learning Coordinator, Tourism and Hospitality Management, Mount Saint Vincent University, EMF Rm. 121, 166

Bedford Hwy., Halifax, Nova Scotia B3M 2J6, Canada; Telephone: 902-457-6511; Fax: 902-457-2618.

INDIVIDUAL COURSES

Mount Saint Vincent University offers individual for-credit courses in: allied health (undergraduate); business/management (undergraduate); tourism (undergraduate).

MURRAY STATE UNIVERSITY
MURRAY, KS 42071

Murray State University first offered a degree program via distance education in 1991.
Total enrollment in distance education programs (1992–93): 25.

_____

Murray State University uses interactive television to deliver courses and one degree program (M.S.N.) to three sites within a 100-mile radius of the campus.

DEGREE PROGRAM

NURSING
Master of Science in Nursing. A 30-semester-hour master's program.

Requirements: Same as for on-campus students.

Degree/Certificate Awarded: Master's—M.S.N.

Availability: Open to RNs with a B.S.N.; 18-county service area.

Primary Methods of Course Delivery and Response: Compressed-video television; fax.

Accreditation: National League for Nursing.

For more information, contact: Dr. Marcia Hobbs, Department Chair, Nursing Department, Murray State University, 1 Murray St., Murray, KS 42071; Telephone: 502-762-2193; Fax: 502-762-6662.

INDIVIDUAL COURSES

Murray State University offers individual for-credit courses in: accounting (undergraduate and graduate); allied health (undergraduate and graduate); business/management (undergraduate and graduate); criminal justice/law (undergraduate); environmental health and safety (undergraduate); foreign languages (undergraduate); liberal arts/general studies (undergraduate); nursing (undergraduate and graduate); teacher education (graduate).

NATIONAL TECHNOLOGICAL UNIVERSITY
FORT COLLINS, CO 80526

National Technological University first offered a degree program via distance education in 1984.

Total enrollment in distance education programs (1992–93): 5,077.

Number graduating from distance programs (spring 1992): 118.

National Technological University serves the educational needs of graduate engineers, technical professionals, and managers and awards master's-level degrees and certificates. The programs offered by National Technological University draw upon approved course offerings from 43 member universities, which arrange for transfer of course credits and grades to National Technological University. Enrollees in National Technological University programs generally do not leave their workplace to participate in the instructional programs. Each National Technological University site is operated by a sponsoring organization following guidelines provided by National Technological University.

DEGREE PROGRAMS

COMPUTER ENGINEERING
Consists of 30 semester credits (or the equivalent quarter credits) distributed through four broad categories: core, depth, breadth, and elective courses.

Requirements: B.S. in engineering from an Accreditation Board for Engineering and Technology–accredited engineering program; 2.9 GPA.

Degree/Certificate Awarded: Master's—M.S.

Availability: Open to corporate, government and university subscribers in the U.S., Canada, and Mexico.

Primary Methods of Course Delivery and Response: Electronic mail; fax; satellite television; videocassette; videoconferencing.

For more information, contact: Douglas Yeager, Marketing Vice President, Marketing/Customer Service, National Technological University, 700 Centre Ave., Fort Collins, CO 80526; Telephone: 303-495-6414; Fax: 303-484-0668; Internet: DOUG.YEAGER@NTUPUB.NTU.EDU

COMPUTER SCIENCE
Consists of 30 semester credits (or the equivalent quarter credits) distributed through four broad categories: core, depth, breadth, and elective courses.

Requirements: B.S. in computer science; 2.9 GPA.

Degree/Certificate Awarded: Master's—M.S.

Availability: Open to corporate, government, and university subscribers in the U.S., Canada, and Mexico.

Primary Methods of Course Delivery and Response: Electronic mail; fax; satellite television; videocassette; videoconferencing.

For more information, contact: Douglas Yeager, Marketing Vice President, Marketing/Customer Service, National Technological University, 700 Centre Ave., Fort Collins, CO 80526; Telephone: 303-495-6414; Fax: 303-484-0668; Internet: DOUG.YEAGER@NTUPUB.NTU.EDU

ELECTRICAL ENGINEERING
Consists of 33 graduate semester credits (or the equivalent number of quarter credits) distributed over three broad categories: depth, breadth, and elective.

Requirements: B.S. in engineering from an Accreditation Board for Engineering and Technology–accredited engineering program; 2.9 GPA.

Degree/Certificate Awarded: Master's—M.S.

Availability: Open to corporate, government, and university subscribers in the U.S., Canada, and Mexico.

Primary Methods of Course Delivery and Response: Electronic mail; fax; satellite television; videocassette; videoconferencing.

For more information, contact: Douglas Yeager, Marketing Vice President, Marketing/Customer Service, National Technological University, 700 Centre Ave., Fort Collins, CO 80526; Telephone: 303-495-6414; Fax: 303-484-0668; Internet: DOUG.YEAGER@NTUPUB.NTU.EDU

ENGINEERING MANAGEMENT
Program consists of a minimum of 33 semester credits distributed among two broad categories of courses: core (including a Capstone Project Course) and elective.

Requirements: B.S. in engineering from an Accreditation Board for Engineering and Technology–accredited engineering program; 2.9 GPA.

Degree/Certificate Awarded: Master's—M.S.

Availability: Open to corporate, government, and university subscribers in the U.S., Canada, and Mexico.

Primary Methods of Course Delivery and Response: Electronic mail; fax; satellite television; videocassette; videoconferencing.

For more information, contact: Douglas Yeager, Marketing Vice President, Marketing/Customer Service, National Technological University, 700 Centre Ave., Fort Collins, CO 80526; Telephone: 303-495-6414; Fax: 303-484-0668; Internet: DOUG.YEAGER@NTUPUB.NTU.EDU

HAZARDOUS WASTE MANAGEMENT
Program consists of 33 semester credits including four required courses, two depth areas in management and treatment/technical subjects, a three-credit Capstone Project Course, and elective courses from a variety of support areas.

Requirements: B.S. in engineering or hard sciences (e.g., biology, chemistry, physics, geology); college math courses through ordinary differential equations; 2.9 GPA.

Degree/Certificate Awarded: Master's—M.S.

Availability: Open to corporate, government, and university subscribers in the U.S., Canada, and Mexico.

Primary Methods of Course Delivery and Response: Electronic mail; fax; satellite television; videocassette; videoconferencing.

For more information, contact: Douglas Yeager, Marketing Vice President, Marketing/Customer Service, National Technological University, 700 Centre Ave., Fort Collins, CO 80526; Telephone: 303-495-6414; Fax: 303-484-0668; Internet: DOUG.YEAGER@NTUPUB.NTU.EDU

HEALTH PHYSICS
Consists of 32 semester credits—21 credits from core courses and seven from elective courses.

Requirements: B.S. from an accredited university, preferably in one of the sciences; 3.0 GPA; verbal and quantitative GRE score in at least the 80th percentile; three letters of recommendation; two university semester courses in chemistry and in physics and one in biology; mathematics through integral calculus and differential equations strongly recommended.

Degree/Certificate Awarded: Master's—M.S.

Availability: Open to corporate, government, and university subscribers in the U.S., Canada, and Mexico.

Primary Methods of Course Delivery and Response: Electronic mail; fax; satellite television; videocassette; videoconferencing.

On-Campus Component: Two on-campus laboratory courses, usually in the summer.

For more information, contact: Douglas Yeager, Marketing Vice President, Marketing/Customer Service, National Technological University, 700 Centre Ave., Fort Collins, CO 80526; Telephone: 303-495-6414; Fax: 303-484-0668; Internet: DOUG.YEAGER@NTUPUB.NTU.EDU

MANAGEMENT OF TECHNOLOGY
Consists of 45 credits distributed over a wide interdisciplinary range, including economics, accounting, manufacturing, finance, marketing, and research and development management.

Requirements: B.S.; 2.9 GPA; knowledge of calculus, economics, and statistics; management sponsorship; at least two years work experience in an engineering environment.

Degree/Certificate Awarded: Master's—M.S.

Availability: Open to corporate, government, and university subscribers in the U.S., Canada, and Mexico.

Primary Methods of Course Delivery and Response: Electronic mail; fax; satellite television; videocassette; videoconferencing.

On-Campus Component: Six one-week residencies.

For more information, contact: Douglas Yeager, Marketing Vice President, Marketing/Customer Service, National Technological University, 700 Centre Ave.,

Fort Collins, CO 80526; Telephone: 303-495-6414; Fax: 303-484-0668; Internet: DOUG.YEAGER@NTUPUB.NTU.EDU

MANUFACTURING SYSTEMS ENGINEERING
Consists of 33 semester credits (or the equivalent quarter credits) in core, depth, breadth, and elective courses.

Requirements: B.S. in engineering from an Accreditation Board for Engineering and Technology–accredited engineering program; 2.9 GPA.

Degree/Certificate Awarded: Master's—M.S.

Availability: Open to corporate, government, and university subscribers in the U.S., Canada, and Mexico.

Primary Methods of Course Delivery and Response: Electronic mail; fax; satellite television; videocassette; videoconferencing.

For more information, contact: Douglas Yeager, Marketing Vice President, Marketing/Customer Service, National Technological University, 700 Centre Ave., Fort Collins, CO 80526; Telephone: 303-495-6414; Fax: 303-484-0668; Internet: DOUG.YEAGER@NTUPUB.NTU.EDU

MATERIALS SCIENCE AND ENGINEERING
Consists of 33 semester credit hours, including three semester credit hours for an individual project course.

Requirements: B.S. in materials science or engineering from an Accreditation Board for Engineering and Technology–accredited institution; 3.0 GPA.

Degree/Certificate Awarded: Master's—M.S.

Availability: Open to corporate, government, and university subscribers in the U.S., Canada, and Mexico.

Primary Methods of Course Delivery and Response: Electronic mail; fax; satellite television; videocassette; videoconferencing.

For more information, contact: Douglas Yeager, Marketing Vice President, Marketing/Customer Service, National Technological University, 700 Centre Ave., Fort Collins, CO 80526; Telephone: 303-495-6414; Fax: 303-484-0668; Internet: DOUG.YEAGER@NTUPUB.NTU.EDU

SOFTWARE ENGINEERING
Consists of 33 semester credits (or the equivalent quarter credits) distributed through four core, depth, breadth, and elective courses.

Requirements: B.S. in computer science, computer engineering, or an accredited engineering program with a minor in computing systems; 2.9 GPA; demonstrated knowledge of key topics.

Degree/Certificate Awarded: Master's—M.S.

Availability: Open to corporate, government, and university subscribers in the U.S., Canada, and Mexico.

Primary Methods of Course Delivery and Response: Electronic mail; fax; satellite television; videocassette; videoconferencing.

For more information, contact: Douglas Yeager, Marketing Vice President, Marketing/Customer Service, National Technological University, 700 Centre Ave., Fort Collins, CO 80526; Telephone: 303-495-6414; Fax: 303-484-0668; Internet: DOUG.YEAGER@NTUPUB.NTU.EDU

INDIVIDUAL COURSES

National Technological University offers individual for-credit courses in: computer science (graduate); engineering (graduate); environmental health and safety (graduate); foreign languages (graduate).

NEW JERSEY INSTITUTE OF TECHNOLOGY
NEWARK, NJ 07102

The New Jersey Institute of Technology first offered a degree program via distance education in 1985.
Total enrollment in distance education programs (1992–93): 1,000.

The New Jersey Institute of Technology's distance learning programs use a combination of delivery methods, including video supported by computerized conferencing. NJIT produces 82 percent of the courses it offers in-house. Faculty are responsible for course content, integrity, and mentoring.

DEGREE PROGRAM

INFORMATION SYSTEMS
Bachelor of Arts in Information Systems via Distance Learning. Application of computing and information systems principles to business, industrial, and managerial problems.

Requirements: Same as for on-campus students.

Degree/Certificate Awarded: Bachelor's—B.A.I.S..

Availability: Open to the public; national.

Primary Methods of Course Delivery and Response: computer conferencing; videocassette.

For more information, contact: Leon Jololian, Director of Curriculum and Instruction, Computer and Information Science, New Jersey Institute of Technology, University Heights, Newark, NJ 07102-1982; Telephone: 201-596-2871; Fax: 201-596-5777; Internet: Leon@Hertz.NJIT.EDU.

INDIVIDUAL COURSES

The New Jersey Institute of Technology offers individual for-credit courses in: business/management (undergraduate and graduate); chemistry (undergraduate and graduate); computer science (undergraduate and graduate); engineering (graduate); environmental health and safety (graduate); liberal arts/general studies (undergraduate); mathematics (undergraduate and graduate); physics (undergraduate and graduate).

NEW YORK INSTITUTE OF TECHNOLOGY
OLD WESTBURY, NY 11568-0170

New York Institute of Technology first offered a degree program via distance education in 1983.

Total enrollment in distance education programs (1992–93): 125.

Number graduating from distance programs (spring 1992): 10.

The On-Line Campus, the distance learning program of the New York Institute of Technology, is a fully accredited program that offers bachelor's degrees in behavioral sciences, business administration, and interdisciplinary studies. Courses can be accessed using a personal computer (IBM compatible or Macintosh) and a modem. The program offers students time flexibility, allowing them to log on at their convenience. Students can complete their degree from start to finish without attending any of NYIT's conventional campuses.

DEGREE PROGRAMS

BEHAVIORAL SCIENCES, BUSINESS ADMINISTRATION, AND INTERDISCIPLINARY STUDIES
Bachelor's degree programs.

Requirements: Open admission.

Degree/Certificate Awarded: Bachelor's—B.S., B.A., B.P.S.

Availability: Open to the public; national.

Primary Methods of Course Delivery and Response: Computer conferencing.

On-Campus Component: None.

Accreditation: Middle States Association.

For more information, contact: Dr. Marshall Kremers, Director, On-Line Campus, New York Institute of Technology, Rm. 417, Old Westbury, NY 11568; Telephone: 800-222-NYIT; Fax: 516-484-8327.

INDIVIDUAL COURSES

New York Institute of Technology offers individual for-credit courses in: accounting (undergraduate); behavioral sciences (undergraduate)—psychology, sociology, community mental health; business/management (undergraduate); criminal justice/law (undergraduate); liberal arts/general studies (undergraduate).

NEW YORK UNIVERSITY
NEW YORK, NY 10011

New York University first offered a degree program via distance education in 1992.

Total enrollment in distance education programs (1992–93): 18.

Number graduating from distance programs (spring 1992): 8.

The Virtual College is an on-line graduate teleprogram that trains managers and professionals to both design and work within electronic environments that connect people as well as computers. The teleprogram provides students with a working knowledge of systems analysis and design, project management, and virtual work-group communications. Using their home or office personal computers and the Lotus Notes groupware package, students and faculty collaborate over national data networks to design and build business applications for their own and case study organizations. Through the Virtual College, students receive instruction, interview clients, conduct analyses, resolve problems, and complete projects—all largely at their own convenience. The teleprogram provides an interactive instructional environment of data, graphics, audio, and video.

DEGREE PROGRAM

MANAGEMENT/COMPUTER SCIENCE
The Virtual College. On-line teleprogram covering information systems analysis, project management, and group communications.

Requirements: Bachelor's degree.

Degree/Certificate Awarded: Postsecondary certificate.

Availability: Open to the public; national.

Primary Methods of Course Delivery and Response: Compressed-video television; computer conferencing; electronic mail.

For more information, contact: Richard Vigilante, Director, Information Technologies Institute, New York University, 48 Cooper Square, New York, NY 10003; Telephone: 212-998-7190; Fax: 212-995-4131; Internet: vigilante@acfcluster.nyu.edu.

INDIVIDUAL COURSES

New York University offers individual for-credit courses in: business/management (graduate); computer science (graduate).

NORTH DAKOTA STATE UNIVERSITY
FARGO, ND 58105

North Dakota State University first offered a degree program via distance education in 1992.

Courses are delivered to designated off-campus sites by a two-way interactive video network (IVN) sponsored and coordinated by the North Dakota University Systems. The sites also are connected by telephones and fax machines. For some courses, in addition to class time on the network, students and faculty correspond by electronic mail. Students may also gain access to a nationwide library network via computer. In addition to courses leading to degrees, the system offers both credit and noncredit programs as requested.

DEGREE PROGRAMS

COUNSELOR EDUCATION
Master's degree program in counseling with specializations in school, chemical, and clinical counseling as well as a general focus.

Requirements: Same as for on-campus graduate students; MAT; CET; personal interview.

Degree/Certificate Awarded: Master's—M.Ed., M.S.

Availability: Open to the public; state-designated sites.

Primary Methods of Course Delivery and Response: Two-way interactive video.

On-Campus Component: Varies according to course and program specialization.

For more information, contact: Robert Nielsen, Associate Professor, School of Education, North Dakota State University, Fargo, ND 58105; Telephone: 701-237-7676.

EDUCATIONAL ADMINISTRATION
Tri-College Education Specialist Program. Post-master's-level graduate program. Five tracks available, including elementary and secondary school principal, community education, and superintendency.

Requirements: Master's degree; MAT; CET; GRE.

Degree/Certificate Awarded: Postsecondary certificate—Specialist.

Consortium Affiliation: Tri-College University, North Dakota State University, Fargo.

Availability: Open to the public; state-designated sites.

Primary Methods of Course Delivery and Response: Two-way interactive video.

On-Campus Component: Varies by course.

Accreditation: National Council for Accreditation of Teacher Education.

For more information, contact: Lawrence Anderson, Chair, Educational Administration, North Dakota State University, Fargo, ND 58105; Telephone: 701-237-8170.

LIBERAL ARTS/GENERAL STUDIES
Bachelor of University Studies. Permits students to tailor their own degree with the approval of the Program Review Committee. May grant experiential credit.

Requirements: Same as for on-campus students.

Degree/Certificate Awarded: Bachelor's—B.U.S.

Availability: Open to the public; state-designated sites.

Primary Methods of Course Delivery and Response: Two-way interactive video.

On-Campus Component: Varies by program.

For more information, contact: Roger Kerns, Dean, College of University Studies, North Dakota State University, Fargo, ND 58105; Telephone: 701-237-7014.

INDIVIDUAL COURSES
North Dakota State University offers individual for-credit courses in: liberal arts/general studies (undergraduate); teacher education (graduate).

NORTHERN ARIZONA UNIVERSITY
FLAGSTAFF, AZ 86011

Northern Arizona University first offered a degree program via distance education in 1990.

Total enrollment in distance education programs (1992–93): 1,200.

At Northern Arizona University–Yuma, Interactive Video Instruction utilizes instantaneous two-way audio/television communication to electronically link a class in Yuma with a class on the Flagstaff campus. Courses are taught simultaneously, and both groups of students can ask questions and interact with their professor or classmates as if all students were together at one site.

DEGREE PROGRAMS

EDUCATION
Master of Education. A 36-hour program with an emphasis in elementary or secondary education, educational leadership, or bilingual/multicultural education.

Requirements: Must be admitted as a degree-seeking graduate student and meet program requirements.

Degree/Certificate Awarded: Master's—M.Ed.

Availability: Open to the public; statewide.

Primary Method of Course Delivery and Response: Fully interactive television delivered via microwave.

On-Campus Component: Varies by campus.

For more information, contact: Dr. Gus Cotera, Executive Director, Northern Arizona University–Yuma, P.O. Box 6235, Yuma, AZ 85366; Telephone: 602-344-7721; Fax: 602-344-7743.

EDUCATION
Administrative Certification. A school (K-12) administration certification program.

Requirements: Mimimum three years certified classroom teaching.

Degree/Certificate Awarded: Postsecondary certificate.

Availability: Open to the public; statewide.

Primary Method of Course Delivery and Response: Fully interactive television delivered via microwave.

On-Campus Component: Varies by campus.

For more information, contact: Dr. Gus Cotera, Executive Director, Northern Arizona University–Yuma, P.O. Box 6235, Yuma, AZ 85366; Telephone: 602-344-7721; Fax: 602-344-7743.

LIBERAL STUDIES
Bachelor of Arts in Liberal Studies. A liberal arts degree with an interdisciplinary focus.

Requirements: Same as for on-campus students; must be admitted as a degree-seeking student.

Degree/Certificate Awarded: Postsecondary certificate, bachelor's—B.A.

Availability: Open to the public; statewide.

Primary Method of Course Delivery and Response: Fully interactive television delivered via microwave.

On-Campus Component: Varies by campus.

For more information, contact: Dr. Gus Cotera, Executive Director, Northern Arizona University–Yuma, P.O. Box 6235, Yuma, AZ 85366; Telephone: 602-344-7721; Fax: 602-344-7743.

INDIVIDUAL COURSES

Northern Arizona University offers individual for-credit courses in: accounting (undergraduate); allied health (undergraduate); business/management (undergraduate); criminal justice/law (undergraduate); engineering (undergraduate); liberal arts/general studies (undergraduate); nursing (undergraduate).

OKLAHOMA STATE UNIVERSITY
STILLWATER, OK 74078

Oklahoma State University first offered a degree program via distance education in 1990.

Total enrollment in distance education programs (1992–93): 373.

Number graduating from distance programs (spring 1992): 7.

At Oklahoma State University, regular faculty members provide distance instruction that is equivalent to what is offered on the main campus. The most current technologies are employed to offer high-quality responsive programs.

DEGREE PROGRAMS

ELECTRICAL ENGINEERING
Master's Degree in Electrical Engineering. Degree is delivered to industry via compressed digital television (in Oklahoma) and via satellite through the National Technological University.

Requirements: Same as for on-campus students.

Degree/Certificate Awarded: Master's—M.S.E.E.

Consortium Affiliation: National Technological University throughout the U.S., Mexico, and Canada.

Availability: Open to corporate subscribers; national.

Primary Methods of Course Delivery and Response: Compressed-video television; fax; satellite television.

For more information, contact: Bill Cooper, Director of Engineering Extension, Oklahoma State University, 512 Engineering North, Stillwater, OK 74078; Telephone: 405-744-5146; Fax: 405-744-5033; Internet: bcooper@master.ceat.okstate.edu.

MECHANICAL ENGINEERING
Master's Degree in Mechanical Engineering. Degree is delivered to industry via compressed digital television.

Requirements: Same as for on-campus students.

Degree/Certificate Awarded: Master's—M.S.M.E.

Availability: Open to corporate subscribers; statewide.

Primary Methods of Course Delivery and Response: Compressed-video television; fax.

For more information, contact: Bill Cooper, Director of Engineering Extension, Oklahoma State University, 512 Engineering North, Stillwater, OK 74078; Telephone: 405-744-5146; Fax: 405-744-5033; Internet: bcooper@master.ceat.okstate.edu.

CHEMICAL ENGINEERING

Master's Degree in Chemical Engineering. Degree is delivered to industry via compressed digital television.

Requirements: Same as for on-campus students.

Degree/Certificate Awarded: Master's—M.S.Ch.E.

Availability: Open to corporate subscribers; statewide.

Primary Methods of Course Delivery and Response: Compressed-video television; fax.

For more information, contact: Bill Cooper, Director of Engineering Extension, Oklahoma State University, 512 Engineering North, Stillwater, OK 74078; Telephone: 405-744-5146; Fax: 405-744-5033; Internet: bcooper@master.ceat.okstate.edu.

ELECTRICAL ENGINEERING

Electrical Engineering Bridging Program. Undergraduate course to prepare students for electrical engineering graduate studies.

Requirements: B.S. in engineering, mathematics, or science.

Availability: Open to corporate subscribers; statewide.

Primary Methods of Course Delivery and Response: Compressed-video television; fax.

Accreditation: Courses are part of an Accreditation Board for Engineering and Technology–accredited B.S.E.E. program.

For more information, contact: Bill Cooper, Director of Engineering Extension, Oklahoma State University, 512 Engineering North, Stillwater, OK 74078; Telephone: 405-744-5146; Fax: 405-744-5033; Internet: bcooper@master.ceat.okstate.edu.

BUSINESS ADMINISTRATION

Corporate M.B.A. Program. Degree program comprising 48 credit hours in management, marketing, and finance.

Requirements: Bachelor's degree; GMAT; calculus and PC proficiency.

Degree/Certificate Awarded: Master's—M.B.A.

Availability: Open to corporate subscribers; statewide.

Primary Methods of Course Delivery and Response: Compressed-video television.

On-Campus Component: Six credit hours (complete 12 seven-hour Saturday seminars in two years).

Accreditation: American Assembly of Collegiate Schools of Business.

For more information, contact: Karen Flock, Manager, Extension Programs, Business Extension, Oklahoma State University, 215 College of Business, Stillwater, OK 74078; Telephone: 405-744-5208; Fax: 405-744-6143.

INDIVIDUAL COURSES

Oklahoma State University offers individual for-credit courses in: accounting (graduate); business/management (graduate); computer science (graduate); engineering (graduate); liberal arts/general studies (graduate).

OLD DOMINION UNIVERSITY

NORFOLK, VA 23529

Old Dominion University first offered a degree program via distance education in 1985.

Total enrollment in distance education programs (1992–93): 2,100.

Number graduating from distance programs (spring 1992): 44.

Bachelor's degree programs are primarily offered in cooperation with community colleges in a 2 + 2 arrangement. All programs utilize a variety of techniques, and some courses are global with international feeds.

DEGREE PROGRAMS

ENGINEERING MANAGEMENT

Master of Science, Engineering Management. Builds on concepts in systems science and systems engineering. Oriented toward design and management of technical projects, complex operations, and technology-based organizations.

Requirements: Bachelor's degree from an Accreditation Board for Engineering and Technology–accredited program in engineering or engineering technology, or an accredited program in applied science or applied mathematics; 3.0 GPA; background in advanced mathematics, including calculus, differential equations, and matrix algebra; minimum 450 verbal, 550 quantitative, 400 analytical GRE with an overall combined score of 1500; 550 TOEFL; two letters of recommendation (preferably one from an employer and one from a former professor); a brief written statement of career objectives; two years full-time work experience in an engineering environment since graduation.

Degree/Certificate Awarded: Master's—M.E.M.

Consortium Affiliation: Virginia Cooperative Graduate Engineering Program.

Availability: Open to the public; regional.

Primary Methods of Course Delivery and Response: Closed-circuit television; fax; public television; satellite television; teleconferencing; telephone.

Accreditation: Southern Association of Colleges and Schools.

For more information, contact: Billie M. Reed, Graduate Program Director, Engineering Management, Old Dominion University, Engineering Management Bldg., 4th St., Norfolk, VA 23529; Telephone: 804-683-4842; Fax: 804-683-5640.

CIVIL AND ENVIRONMENTAL ENGINEERING

Master's in Civil and Environmental Engineering. A 33-credit program in environmental, structural, coastal, geotechnical, or water resources engineering.

Requirements: B.S. in civil or environmental engineering; 2.75 overall GPA; 3.0 GPA in major; GRE.

Degree/Certificate Awarded: Master's—M.S.

Availability: Open to the public; regional.

Primary Methods of Course Delivery and Response: Cable television; closed-circuit television, electronic mail; fax; ITFS; microwave; satellite television; telephone; videocassette; videoconferencing.

Accreditation: Southern Association of Colleges and Schools.

For more information, contact: Dr. A. Osman Akan, Graduate Program Director, Civil Engineering, Old Dominion University, 135 Kaufman/Duckworth Hall, Norfolk, VA 23529; Telephone: 804-683-3753; Fax: 804-683-5354.

ELECTRICAL AND COMPUTER ENGINEERING
Master's in Electrical and Computer Engineering. Advanced courses in electrical and computer engineering design, application, and research.

Requirements: B.S.E.E. from an accredited institution; 3.0 GPA.

Degree/Certificate Awarded: Master's—M.S.

Availability: Open to the public; regional.

Primary Methods of Course Delivery and Response: Cable television; closed-circuit television, electronic mail; fax; ITFS; microwave; satellite television; telephone; videocassette; videoconferencing.

Accreditation: Southern Association of Colleges and Schools.

For more information, contact: Dr. Vishnu K. Lakdawala, Graduate Program Director, Electrical and Computer Engineering, Old Dominion University, 321 Kaufman/Duckworth Hall, Norfolk, VA 23529; Telephone: 804-683-4665; Fax: 804-683-3220; Internet: VKL100F@EEFS01.EE.ODU.EDU.

ELECTRICAL ENGINEERING
Electrical Engineering Technology. Advanced courses in the field along with general education.

Requirements: Associate degree.

Degree/Certificate Awarded: Bachelor's—B.S.

Availability: Open to the public; statewide.

Primary Methods of Course Delivery and Response: Closed-circuit television, fax; fiber; ITFS; microwave; public television; satellite television; teleconferencing; telephone.

Accreditation: Southern Association of Colleges and Schools, Technical Accreditation Commission of the Accreditation Board for Engineering and Technology.

For more information, contact: Dr. William D. Stanley, Program Director, Electrical Engineering Technology, Old Dominion University, 211 Kaufman/Duckworth Hall, Norfolk, VA 23529; Telephone: 804-683-3775; Fax: 804-683-5655.

MECHANICAL ENGINEERING
Bachelor of Science in Mechanical Engineering Technology. Upper-division curriculum offered in a combination of live and televised courses for part-time students.

Requirements: Associate degree.

Degree/Certificate Awarded: Bachelor's—B.S.

Availability: Open to the public; statewide.

Primary Methods of Course Delivery and Response: Closed-circuit television; fax; public television; satellite television; teleconferencing; telephone.

Accreditation: Southern Association of Colleges and Schools, Technical Accreditation Commission of the Accreditation Board for Engineering and Technology.

For more information, contact: Dr. Alok K. Verma, Program Director, Mechanical Engineering Technology, Old Dominion University, Norfolk, VA 23529; Telephone: 804-683-3766; Fax: 804-683-5655.

MECHANICAL ENGINEERING
Master of Science in Mechanical Engineering and Mechanics.

Requirements: Accredited B.S.

Degree/Certificate Awarded: Master's—M.S.

Availability: Open to the public.

Primary Methods of Course Delivery and Response: Closed-circuit television; fax; public television; satellite television; teleconferencing; telephone.

Accreditation: Southern Association of Colleges and Schools.

For more information, contact: Dr. Oktay Baysal, Graduate Program Director, Mechanical Engineering and Mechanics, Old Dominion University, 241 Kaufman/Duckworth Hall, Norfolk, VA 23529; Telephone: 804-683-3720; Fax: 807-683-5344.

NURSING
Master of Science in Nursing. Expertise in theory, research, and advanced practice.

Requirements: MAT; 3.0 undergraduate GPA in nursing and 2.5 overall GPA; undergraduate statistics course; physical assessment component.

Degree/Certificate Awarded: Master's—M.S.N.

Availability: Open to RNs with B.S.N. or equivalent; statewide.

Primary Methods of Course Delivery and Response: Cable television; closed-circuit television; electronic mail; fax; fiber; ITFS, microwave; satellite television; telephone; videocassette; videoconferencing.

Accreditation: Southern Association of Colleges and Schools.

For more information, contact: Dr. Betty Alexy, Graduate Program Director, Nursing, Old Dominion University, Norfolk, VA 23529; Telephone: 804-683-5257; Fax: 804-683-5253.

NURSING
Bachelor of Science in Nursing. Prepares men and women to be beginning

practitioners of professional nursing and qualify for first-level positions in a variety of health settings.

Requirements: University admission; prerequisite courses.

Degree/Certificate Awarded: Bachelor's—B.S.N.

Availability: Open to the public; regional.

Primary Methods of Course Delivery and Response: Closed-circuit television; fax; public television; satellite television; teleconferencing; telephone.

Accreditation: Southern Association of Colleges and Schools, Virginia State Board of Nursing, and National League for Nursing.

For more information, contact: Dr. Brenda S. Nichols, Chairman, Nursing, Old Dominion University, Norfolk, VA 23529; Telephone: 804-683-4299; Fax: 804-683-5253.

INDIVIDUAL COURSES

Old Dominion University offers individual for-credit courses in: accounting (graduate); allied health (undergraduate and graduate); business/management (graduate); computer science (graduate); engineering (undergraduate and graduate); environmental health and safety (undergraduate and graduate); liberal arts/general studies (undergraduate and graduate); nursing (undergraduate and graduate); teacher education (graduate).

OREGON STATE UNIVERSITY
CORVALLIS, OR 97331

Oregon State University first offered a degree program via distance education in 1991.
Total enrollment in distance education programs (1992–93): 200.

DEGREE PROGRAM

LIBERAL STUDIES
Bachelor's in Liberal Studies. Interdisciplinary program that prepares students to function in a multicultural society.

Requirements: High school diploma or associate degree or equivalent.

Degree/Certificate Awarded: Bachelor's—B.A.

Availability: Open to the public; statewide.

Primary Methods of Course Delivery and Response: Compressed-video television; teleconferencing.

Accreditation: Northwest Association of Schools and Colleges.

For more information, contact: Don Olcott, Assistant Director, Extended Learning Program and Continuing Higher Education Department, Oregon State University, Snell Hall, Rm. 327, Corvallis, OR 97331-1633; Telephone: 503-737-1288; Fax: 503-737-2734; Internet: OLCOTTD@ORST.EDU.

INDIVIDUAL COURSES

Oregon State University offers individual for-credit courses in:
business/management (undergraduate); computer science (undergraduate); engineering (graduate); environmental health and safety (graduate); liberal arts/general studies (undergraduate); teacher education (graduate).

PENNSYLVANIA STATE UNIVERSITY
UNIVERSITY PARK, PA 16802

Pennsylvania State University first offered a degree program via distance education in 1971.

Total enrollment in distance education programs (1992–93): 30,000.

Number graduating from distance programs (spring 1992): 24.

DEGREE PROGRAM

ACOUSTICS
Master's Program in Acoustics. Teaches fundamentals of acoustics as applied to underwater acoustics and engineering principles.

Requirements: Bachelor's degree with strong background in engineering/math; GRE.

Degree/Certificate Awarded: Master's—M.S.

Availability: Open to employees of the U.S. Navy and its contractors; national.

Primary Method of Course Delivery and Response: Compressed-video television.

On-Campus Component: One two-week summer session.

For more information, contact: Professor Alan Stuart, Applied Research Lab, 256 Applied Sciences Bldg., Pennsylvania State University, University Park, PA 16802; Telephone: 814-863-4128.

INDIVIDUAL COURSES

Pennsylvania State University offers individual for-credit courses in: allied health (undergraduate and graduate); business/management (undergraduate); criminal justice/law (undergraduate); engineering (graduate); liberal arts/general studies (undergraduate); nursing (undergraduate).

PORTLAND STATE UNIVERSITY
PORTLAND, OR 97207-0751

Portland State University first offered a degree program via distance education in 1988.

Total enrollment in distance education programs (1992–93): 228.

Number graduating from distance programs (spring 1992): 40.

Portland State University's distance learning program is relatively new but growing, serving mostly Oregon.

DEGREE PROGRAM

BUSINESS ADMINISTRATION
Portland State University Statewide M.B.A. Program. On-campus AACSB-accredited degree delivered via video and telecommunications to 15 off-campus sites throughout Oregon.

Requirements: 2.75 GPA; 450 GMAT.

Degree/Certificate Awarded: Master's—M.B.A.

Availability: Open to the public; statewide.

Primary Methods of Course Delivery and Response: Teleconferencing; videodisc.

On-Campus Component: One full day each term.

Accreditation: American Assembly of Collegiate Schools of Business; Northwest Association of Schools and Colleges.

For more information, contact: Katherine S. Novy, Director, School of Business Administration, Portland State University, P.O. Box 751, Portland, OR 97201; Telephone: 503-725-4822; Fax: 503-725-5850.

INDIVIDUAL COURSES

Portland State University offers individual for-credit courses in: geography (undergraduate); social work (graduate); teacher education (graduate).

PURDUE UNIVERSITY
WEST LAFAYETTE, IN 47907

Purdue University first offered a degree program via distance education in 1958. Total enrollment in distance education programs (1992–93): 1,131.

Number graduating from distance programs (spring 1992): 127.

Graduate courses in engineering and related disciplines are televised as they are being taught on the West Lafayette campus by Purdue engineering faculty. These courses may be taken on a credit or audit basis. Qualified engineers may apply for admission to the graduate school and, upon admission, work toward one of several master's degrees that may be earned entirely through televised courses. Courses are televised during the day and are normally 15 weeks long. A wide variety of noncredit videotaped courses and teleconferences are also broadcast.

DEGREE PROGRAMS

ENGINEERING
Master of Science in Engineering. Interdisciplinary program emphasizing basic engineering science, designed to meet the specific needs of engineers employed in industry.

Requirements: Bachelor's degree in engineering or a related area.

Degree/Certificate Awarded: Master's—M.S.E.

Consortium Affiliation: National Technological University, Fort Collins, CO.

Availability: Open to the public; national.

Primary Method of Course Delivery and Response: Satellite television.

For more information, contact: Dr. Philip Swain, Director, Continuing Engineering Education, Purdue University, 1575 Civil Engineering Bldg., West Lafayette, IN 47907; Telephone: 317-494-0212; Fax: 317-496-1196; Internet: swain@ecn.purdue.edu.

INDUSTRIAL ENGINEERING
Master of Science in Industrial Engineering. Interdisciplinary program emphasizing basic engineering science, designed to meet the specific needs of engineers employed in industry.

Requirements: Bachelor's degree in engineering or a related area.

Degree/Certificate Awarded: Master's—M.S.I.E.

Consortium Affiliation: National Technological University, Fort Collins, CO.

Availability: Open to the public; national.

Primary Method of Course Delivery and Response: Satellite television.

For more information, contact: Dr. Philip Swain, Director, Continuing Engineering Education, Purdue University, 1575 Civil Engineering Bldg., West Lafayette, IN

47907; Telephone: 317-494-0212; Fax: 317-496-1196; Internet: swain@ecn.purdue.edu.

ELECTRICAL ENGINEERING

Master of Science in Electrical Engineering. Interdisciplinary program emphasizing basic engineering science, designed to meet the specific needs of engineers employed in industry.

Requirements: Bachelor's degree in engineering or a related area.

Degree/Certificate Awarded: Master's—M.S.E.E.

Consortium Affiliation: National Technological University, Fort Collins, CO.

Availability: Open to the public; national.

Primary Method of Course Delivery and Response: Satellite television.

For more information, contact: Dr. Philip Swain, Director, Continuing Engineering Education, Purdue University, 1575 Civil Engineering Bldg., West Lafayette, IN 47907; Telephone: 317-494-0212; Fax: 317-496-1196; Internet: swain@ecn.purdue.edu.

MECHANICAL ENGINEERING

Master of Science in Mechanical Engineering. Interdisciplinary program emphasizing basic engineering science, designed to meet the specific needs of engineers employed in industry.

Requirements: Bachelor's degree in engineering or a related area.

Degree/Certificate Awarded: Master's—M.S.M.E.

Consortium Affiliation: National Technological University, Fort Collins, CO.

Availability: Open to the public; national.

Primary Method of Course Delivery and Response: Satellite television.

For more information, contact: Dr. Philip Swain, Director, Continuing Engineering Education, Purdue University, 1575 Civil Engineering Bldg., West Lafayette, IN 47907; Telephone: 317-494-0212; Fax: 317-496-1196; Internet: swain@ecn.purdue.edu.

CIVIL ENGINEERING

Master of Science in Civil Engineering. Interdisciplinary program emphasizing basic engineering science, designed to meet the specific needs of engineers employed in industry.

Requirements: Bachelor's degree in engineering or a related area.

Degree/Certificate Awarded: Master's—M.S.C.E.

Consortium Affiliation: National Technological University, Fort Collins, CO.

Availability: Open to the public; national.

Primary Method of Course Delivery and Response: Satellite television.

For more information, contact: Dr. Philip Swain, Director, Continuing Engineering Education, Purdue University, 1575 Civil Engineering Bldg., West Lafayette, IN

47907; Telephone: 317-494-0212; Fax: 317-496-1196; Internet: swain@ecn.purdue.edu.

PHARMACY
Consultant Pharmacy Certificate.

Requirements: B.S. in pharmacy.

Degree/Certificate Awarded: Postsecondary certificate.

Availability: Open to the public; statewide; also offered in Georgia, Michigan, and Louisiana.

Primary Method of Course Delivery and Response: Videocassette.

On-Campus Component: Ten regional workshop sessions.

PHARMACY
Drug Therapy Monitoring Certificate.

Requirements: B.S. in pharmacy.

Degree/Certificate Awarded: Postsecondary certificate.

Availability: Open to the public; statewide; also offered in Ohio.

Primary Method of Course Delivery and Response: Videocassette.

On-Campus Component: Eight regional workshops.

For more information, contact: Jerome Blank, Director of Continuing Education, Pharmacy Practice, Purdue University, Rm. 302, Pharmacy Bldg.–1335, West Lafayette, IN 47907-1335; Telephone: 317-494-1473.

PHARMACY
Nontraditional Pharm.D. Didactic portion offered at a distance; clerkship at hospitals and other practice sites.

Requirements: B.S. in pharmacy.

Degree/Certificate Awarded: Master's—Pharm.D.

Availability: Open to the public; statewide.

Primary Method of Course Delivery and Response: Videocassette.

For more information, contact: Jerome Blank, Director of Continuing Education, Pharmacy Practice, Purdue University, Rm. 302, Pharmacy Bldg.–1335, West Lafayette, IN 47907-1335; Telephone: 317-494-1473.

INDIVIDUAL COURSES

Purdue University offers an individual for-credit course in: engineering (graduate).

REGENT UNIVERSITY
VIRGINIA BEACH, VA 23464

Regent University first offered a degree program via distance education in 1991. Total enrollment in distance education programs (1992–93): 65.

Courses via audiotape, supplemented with study guides and text, provide biblical-based graduate-level management education to students who choose not to attend the traditional classroom.

DEGREE PROGRAMS

MANAGEMENT
Master of Arts Management.

Requirements: Bachelor's degree; 2.5 GPA; GMAT.

Degree/Certificate Awarded: Master's—M.A.M.

Availability: Open to the public; 39 states approved/licensed.

Primary Methods of Course Delivery and Response: Audiocassette.

On-Campus Component: Two one-week periods.

Accreditation: Southern Association of Colleges and Schools.

For more information, contact: Mike Gray, Admissions Coordinator, College of Administration and Management, Regent University, 1000 Centerville Turnpike, Virginia Beach, VA 23464-5041; Telephone: 804-523-7421; Fax: 804-424-7051.

BUSINESS ADMINISTRATION
Master of Business Administration.

Requirements: Bachelor's degree; 2.5 GPA; GMAT.

Degree/Certificate Awarded: Master's—M.B.A.

Availability: Open to the public; 39 states approved/licensed.

Primary Methods of Course Delivery and Response: Audiocassette.

On-Campus Component: Two one-week periods.

Accreditation: Southern Association of Colleges and Schools.

For more information, contact: Mike Gray, Admissions Coordinator, College of Administration and Management, Regent University, 1000 Centerville Tpke., Virginia Beach, VA 23464-5041; Telephone: 804-523-7421; Fax: 804-424-7051.

BIBLICAL STUDIES
Advanced Certificate in Practical Theology.

Requirements: Bachelor's degree; pastoral reference.

Degree/Certificate Awarded: Postsecondary certificate.

Availability: Open to the public; national except where not state approved.

Primary Methods of Course Delivery and Response: Audiocassette.

Accreditation: Southern Association of Colleges and Schools.

For more information, contact: Les Ballard, Assistant Administrator, School of Divinity D.E., Regent University, Virginia Beach, VA 23464; Telephone: 804-523-7668; Fax: 804-424-7051.

INDIVIDUAL COURSES

Regent University offers individual for-credit courses in: accounting (graduate); biblical studies (graduate); business/management (graduate).

RENSSELAER POLYTECHNIC INSTITUTE
TROY, NY 12180

Rensselaer Polytechnic Institute first offered a degree program via distance education in 1987.

Total enrollment in distance education programs (1992–93): 600.

Number graduating from distance programs (spring 1992): 40.

Rensselaer Satellite Video Program provides graduate courses and programs to industrial partners. Master's degree programs are offered in manufacturing systems engineering, microelectronics manufacturing, management of technology, materials engineering, mechanical engineering, and computer science. Four-course continuing education certificates are available in the areas just mentioned and in reliability, robotics and automation, and technical communication. Delivery is by Ku-band satellite. At some locations, courses can be received through interactive compressed video.

DEGREE PROGRAMS

TECHNICAL COMMUNICATION
Master's in Technical Communication.

Requirements: Bachelor's degree; strong academic record and communication skills.

Degree/Certificate Awarded: Master's—M.S.

Availability: Open to corporate subscribers; national.

Primary Methods of Course Delivery and Response: Electronic mail; fax; satellite television; videocassette.

On-Campus Component: None, but six courses are delivered at the industrial site.

For more information, contact: Susan Bray, Director, Rensselaer Satellite Video Program, Continuing Education, Rensselaer Polytechnic Institute, CII 4011, Troy, NY 12180; Telephone: 518-276-8351; Fax: 518-276-8026; Internet: SUSAN_BRAY@MTS.RPI.EDU.

MATERIALS ENGINEERING
Master's in Material Engineering. Disciplinary program consisting of eight courses and project/thesis.

Requirements: Bachelor's degree in engineering/science; strong academic record.

Degree/Certificate Awarded: Master's—M.S.

Availability: Open to corporate subscribers; national.

Primary Methods of Course Delivery and Response: Electronic mail; fax; satellite television; videocassette.

For more information, contact: Susan Bray, Director, Rensselaer Satellite Video

Program, Continuing Education, Rensselaer Polytechnic Institute, CII 4011, Troy, NY 12180; Telephone: 518-276-8351; Fax: 518-276-8026; Internet: SUSAN_BRAY@MTS.RPI.EDU.

MECHANICAL ENGINEERING
Master's in Mechanical Engineering. Disciplinary program consisting of ten courses.

Requirements: Bachelor's degree in mechanical engineering or closely allied field; strong academic record.

Degree/Certificate Awarded: Master's—M.S.

Availability: Open to corporate subscribers; national.

Primary Methods of Course Delivery and Response: Electronic mail; fax; satellite television; videocassette.

For more information, contact: Susan Bray, Director, Rensselaer Satellite Video Program, Continuing Education, Rensselaer Polytechnic Institute, CII 4011, Troy, NY 12180; Telephone: 518-276-8351; Fax: 518-276-8026; Internet: SUSAN_BRAY@MTS.RPI.EDU.

MANUFACTURING SYSTEMS ENGINEERING
Master's in Manufacturing Systems Engineering. Interdisciplinary program leading to an M.S. in engineering science. Concentrations in reliability and robotics and automation.

Requirements: Bachelor's degree in engineering or science; strong academic record.

Degree/Certificate Awarded: Master's—M.S.

Availability: Open to corporate subscribers; national.

Primary Methods of Course Delivery and Response: Compressed satellite television; electronic mail; fax; videocassette.

For more information, contact: Susan Bray, Director, Rensselaer Satellite Video Program, Continuing Education, Rensselaer Polytechnic Institute, CII 4011, Troy, NY 12180; Telephone: 518-276-8351; Fax: 518-276-8026; Internet: SUSAN_BRAY@MTS.RPI.EDU.

COMPUTER SCIENCE
Master's in Computer Science. A disciplinary program consisting of nine courses and a software project.

Requirements: Bachelor's degree; strong math and academic background with courses in data structures and Assembler language programming.

Degree/Certificate Awarded: Master's—M.S.

Availability: Open to corporate subscribers; national.

Primary Methods of Course Delivery and Response: Electronic mail; fax; satellite television; videocassette.

For more information, contact: Susan Bray, Director, Rensselaer Satellite Video Program, Continuing Education, Rensselaer Polytechnic Institute, CII 4011, Troy,

NY 12180; Telephone: 518-276-8351; Fax: 518-276-8026; Internet: SUSAN_BRAY@MTS.RPI.EDU.

MANAGEMENT ENGINEERING
Master's in Management of Technology. Interdisciplinary program leading to an M.S. in engineering science. Designed for individuals with technical background who are assuming management positions in a technological environment.

Requirements: Bachelor's degree in engineering or science; strong math and academic background.

Degree/Certificate Awarded: Master's—M.S.

Availability: Open to corporate subscribers; national.

Primary Methods of Course Delivery and Response: Electronic mail; fax; satellite television; videocassette.

On-Campus Component: None, but two of the ten courses are delivered at the industrial site.

For more information, contact: Susan Bray, Director, Rensselaer Satellite Video Program, Continuing Education, Rensselaer Polytechnic Institute, CII 4011, Troy, NY 12180; Telephone: 518-276-8351; Fax: 518-276-8026; Internet: SUSAN_BRAY@MTS.RPI.EDU.

MICROELECTRONICS MANUFACTURING
Master's in Microelectronics Manufacturing. Interdisciplinary program leading to an M.S. in engineering science. Courses are from electrical engineering, materials engineering, and other disciplines.

Requirements: Bachelor's degree in engineering or science; strong academic record.

Degree/Certificate Awarded: Master's—M.S.

Availability: Open to corporate subscribers; national.

Primary Methods of Course Delivery and Response: Electronic mail; fax; satellite television; videocassette.

For more information, contact: Susan Bray, Director, Rensselaer Satellite Video Program, Continuing Education, Rensselaer Polytechnic Institute, CII 4011, Troy, NY 12180; Telephone: 518-276-8351; Fax: 518-276-8026; Internet: SUSAN_BRAY@MTS.RPI.EDU.

COMPUTER SCIENCE
Certificate. Sequence of four graduate courses in computer science, yielding 12 graduate credits.

Requirements: Bachelor's degree; strong math and academic background including courses in data structures and Assembler language programming.

Degree/Certificate Awarded: Postsecondary certificate.

Availability: Open to corporate subscribers; national.

Primary Methods of Course Delivery and Response: Electronic mail; fax; satellite television; videocassette.

For more information, contact: Susan Bray, Director, Rensselaer Satellite Video Program, Continuing Education, Rensselaer Polytechnic Institute, CII 4011, Troy, NY 12180; Telephone: 518-276-8351; Fax: 518-276-8026; Internet: SUSAN_BRAY@MTS.RPI.EDU.

ROBOTICS AND AUTOMATION
Certificate. Sequence of four graduate courses in robotics and automation, yielding 12 graduate credits.

Requirements: Bachelor's degree in mechanical or electrical engineering; strong academic background including a course in linear systems/control systems.

Degree/Certificate Awarded: Postsecondary certificate.

Availability: Open to corporate subscribers; national.

Primary Methods of Course Delivery and Response: Electronic mail; fax; satellite television; videocassette.

For more information, contact: Susan Bray, Director, Rensselaer Satellite Video Program, Continuing Education, Rensselaer Polytechnic Institute, CII 4011, Troy, NY 12180; Telephone: 518-276-8351; Fax: 518-276-8026; Internet: SUSAN_BRAY@MTS.RPI.EDU.

RELIABILITY
Certificate. Sequence of four graduate courses in reliability, yielding 12 graduate credits.

Requirements: Bachelor's degree in engineering or science; strong academic and math background.

Degree/Certificate Awarded: Postsecondary certificate.

Availability: Open to corporate subscribers; national.

Primary Methods of Course Delivery and Response: Electronic mail; fax; satellite television; videocassette.

For more information, contact: Susan Bray, Director, Rensselaer Satellite Video Program, Continuing Education, Rensselaer Polytechnic Institute, CII 4011, Troy, NY 12180; Telephone: 518-276-8351; Fax: 518-276-8026; Internet: SUSAN_BRAY@MTS.RPI.EDU.

MANUFACTURING SYSTEMS ENGINEERING
Certificate. Sequence of four graduate courses in manufacturing, yielding 12 graduate credits.

Requirements: Bachelor's degree in engineering or science; strong math and academic background.

Degree/Certificate Awarded: Postsecondary certificate.

Availability: Open to corporate subscribers; national.

Primary Methods of Course Delivery and Response: Electronic mail; fax; satellite television; videocassette.

For more information, contact: Susan Bray, Director, Rensselaer Satellite Video Program, Continuing Education, Rensselaer Polytechnic Institute, CII 4011, Troy,

NY 12180; Telephone: 518-276-8351; Fax: 518-276-8026; Internet: SUSAN_BRAY@MTS.RPI.EDU.

MECHANICAL ENGINEERING
Certificate. Sequence of four graduate courses in mechanical engineering, yielding 12 graduate credits.

Requirements: Bachelor's degree in mechanical engineering; strong math and academic record.

Degree/Certificate Awarded: Postsecondary certificate.

Availability: Open to corporate subscribers; national.

Primary Methods of Course Delivery and Response: Electronic mail; fax; satellite television; videocassette.

For more information, contact: Susan Bray, Director, Rensselaer Satellite Video Program, Continuing Education, Rensselaer Polytechnic Institute, CII 4011, Troy, NY 12180; Telephone: 518-276-8351; Fax: 518-276-8026; Internet: SUSAN_BRAY@MTS.RPI.EDU.

MICROELECTRONICS MANUFACTURING
Certificate. Sequence of four graduate courses in microelectronics manufacturing, yielding four graduate credits.

Requirements: Bachelor's degree in engineering or science; strong math and academic background.

Degree/Certificate Awarded: Postsecondary certificate.

Availability: Open to corporate subscribers; national.

Primary Methods of Course Delivery and Response: Electronic mail; fax; satellite television; videocassette.

For more information, contact: Susan Bray, Director, Rensselaer Satellite Video Program, Continuing Education, Rensselaer Polytechnic Institute, CII 4011, Troy, NY 12180; Telephone: 518-276-8351; Fax: 518-276-8026; Internet: SUSAN_BRAY@MTS.RPI.EDU.

MANAGEMENT OF TECHNOLOGY
Certificate. Sequence of four graduate courses in the management of technology, yielding four graduate credits.

Requirements: Bachelor's degree in engineering or science; strong math and academic record.

Degree/Certificate Awarded: Postsecondary certificate.

Availability: Open to corporate subscribers; national.

Primary Methods of Course Delivery and Response: Electronic mail; fax; satellite television; videocassette.

For more information, contact: Susan Bray, Director, Rensselaer Satellite Video Program, Continuing Education, Rensselaer Polytechnic Institute, CII 4011, Troy, NY 12180; Telephone: 518-276-8351; Fax: 518-276-8026; Internet: SUSAN_BRAY@MTS.RPI.EDU.

MATERIALS ENGINEERING

Certificate. Sequence of four graduate courses in materials engineering, yielding 12 graduate credits.

Requirements: Bachelor's degree in engineering or science. Strong math and academic background.

Degree/Certificate Awarded: Postsecondary certificate.

Availability: Open to corporate subscribers; national.

Primary Methods of Course Delivery and Response: Electronic mail; fax; satellite television; videocassette.

For more information, contact: Susan Bray, Director, Rensselaer Satellite Video Program, Continuing Education, Rensselaer Polytechnic Institute, CII 4011, Troy, NY 12180; Telephone: 518-276-8351; Fax: 518-276-8026; Internet: SUSAN_BRAY@MTS.RPI.EDU.

TECHNICAL COMMUNICATION

Certificate. Sequence of four graduate courses in technical communication, yielding 12 graduate credits.

Requirements: Bachelor's degree; strong academic record and communication skills.

Degree/Certificate Awarded: Postsecondary certificate.

Availability: Open to corporate subscribers; national.

Primary Methods of Course Delivery and Response: Electronic mail; fax; satellite television; videocassette.

For more information, contact: Susan Bray, Director, Rensselaer Satellite Video Program, Continuing Education, Rensselaer Polytechnic Institute, CII 4011, Troy, NY 12180; Telephone: 518-276-8351; Fax: 518-276-8026; Internet: SUSAN_BRAY@MTS.RPI.EDU.

INDIVIDUAL COURSES

Rensselaer Polytechnic Institute offers individual for-credit courses in: business/management (graduate); computer science (graduate); engineering (graduate); technical communication (graduate).

RICE UNIVERSITY
HOUSTON, TX 77251

Rice University first offered a degree program via distance education in 1985. Total enrollment in distance education programs (1992–93): 12.

Number graduating from distance programs (spring 1992): 2.

Rice University offers a part-time professional master's degree program in electrical engineering or computer science for local industry.

DEGREE PROGRAM

ENGINEERING AND COMPUTER SCIENCE

Rice Institute for Continuing Engineering Education. Part-time professional master's degree program in electrical engineering or computer science.

Requirements: B.S. in electrical engineering or computer science.

Degree/Certificate Awarded: Master's—M.E.E. or M.C.S.

Availability: Local.

Primary Method of Course Delivery and Response: Educational TV network.

On-Campus Component: Advising, seminars, and some exams.

For more information, contact: Hardy M. Bourland, Associate Dean of Engineering, George R. Brown School of Engineering, Rice University, P.O. Box 1892, Houston, TX 77251; Telephone: 713-527-4955; Fax: 713-285-5300.

INDIVIDUAL COURSES

Rice University offers an individual for-credit course in: engineering (graduate).

ROCHESTER INSTITUTE OF TECHNOLOGY
ROCHESTER, NY 14623-0887

Rochester Institute of Technology first offered a degree program via distance education in 1991.
Total enrollment in distance education programs (1992–93): 2,000.

Number graduating from distance programs (spring 1992): 12.

Rochester Institute of Technology offers highly interactive distance education programs using computer and telecommunications technology including videotape, audiotape, audio conferencing, computer conferencing, electronic mail, and electronic blackboards. Courses are the same as those offered on campus and are taught by the school's on-campus faculty. Rochester Institute of Technology provides phone-in registration, 800 numbers, telephone advising services, mail order for textbooks and videotapes, and a variety of on-line resources, including library services.

DEGREE PROGRAMS

SOFTWARE ENGINEERING
Master of Telecommunications Software Technology. Software engineering principles, telecommunications technology, and software in telecommunications.

Requirements: Bachelor's degree or equivalent; 3.0 GPA.

Degree/Certificate Awarded: Master's—M.S.

Availability: Open to the public; national.

Primary Methods of Course Delivery and Response: Audio conferencing; cable television; computer conferencing; computer diskette; electronic bulletin board; electronic mail; fax; teleconferencing; telephone; videocassette.

Accreditation: Middle States.

For more information, contact: Dr. Peter Lutz, Chairman, Information Technology, Rochester Institute of Technology, P.O. Box 9887, Rochester, NY 14623; Telephone: 800-CALL-RIT; Fax: 716-475-7100; Internet: phl@cs.rit.edu; Bitnet: phlics@ritvax.

ELECTRICAL/MECHANICAL ENGINEERING
Bachelor of Science in Electrical/Mechanical Technology. Interdisciplinary engineering technology program containing core courses in electricity, electronics, materials, mechanics, and manufacturing. Senior elective sequence used to customize program.

Requirements: Associate degree in electrical or mechanical technology or equivalent.

Degree/Certificate Awarded: Bachelor's—B.S.

Availability: Open to the public; community college or industry sites.

Primary Methods of Course Delivery and Response: Audiographics teleconferencing; electronic mail; fax; teleconferencing; videocassette.

On-Campus Component: Within New York State, two courses must be taken on campus. No on-campus requirement outside New York State.

Accreditation: Middle States.

For more information, contact: James Scudder, Associate Director, School of Engineering Technology, Rochester Institute of Technology, P.O. Box 9887, Rochester, NY 14623; Telephone: 800-CALL-RIT; Fax: 716-475-5275; Internet: JFSITE@isc.rit.edu; Bitnet: JFSITE@ritvax.

COMPUTER SCIENCE
M.S. in Software Development and Management. Program focuses on developing software from specification, analysis, and design to testing and implementation.

Requirements: Bachelor's degree or equivalent from an accredited university; 3.0 GPA.

Degree/Certificate Awarded: Master's—M.S.

Availability: Open to the public; national.

Primary Methods of Course Delivery and Response: Audio conferencing; cable television; computer conferencing; computer diskette; electronic bulletin board; electronic mail; fax; public television; teleconferencing; telephone; videocassette.

Accreditation: Middle States.

For more information, contact: Evelyn Rozanski, Graduate Program Chair, Information Technologies, Rochester Institute of Technology, P.O. Box 9887, Rochester, NY 14623; Telephone: 800-CALL-RIT; Fax: 716-475-7100; Internet: EPR@cs.rit.edu; Bitnet: EPRICS@ritvax.

DATA COMMUNICATIONS
Certificate. A three-course sequence providing college-level training for telecommunications professionals and those in related fields.

Requirements: None.

Degree/Certificate Awarded: Postsecondary certificate.

Availability: Open to the public; national.

Primary Methods of Course Delivery and Response: Cable television; computer conferencing; electronic bulletin board; electronic mail; fax; public television; teleconferencing; telephone; videocassette.

For more information, contact: Chris Geith, Program and Market Developer, Distance Learning, Rochester Institute of Technology, P.O. Box 9887, Rochester, NY 14623; Telephone: 800-CALL-RIT; Fax: 716-475-5077; Internet: CMGODL@ritvax.isc.rit.edu; Bitnet: CMGODL@ritvax.

VOICE COMMUNICATIONS
Certificate. A three-course sequence providing college-level training for telecommunications professionals and those in related fields.

Requirements: None.

Degree/Certificate Awarded: Postsecondary certificate.

Availability: Open to the public; national.

Primary Methods of Course Delivery and Response: Cable television; computer conferencing; electronic bulletin board; electronic mail; fax; public television; teleconferencing; telephone; videocassette.

For more information, contact: Chris Geith, Program and Market Developer, Distance Learning, Rochester Institute of Technology, P.O. Box 9887, Rochester, NY 14623; Telephone: 800-CALL-RIT; Fax: 716-475-5077; Internet: CMGODL@ritvax.isc.rit.edu; Bitnet: CMGODL@ritvax.

APPLIED COMPUTING AND COMMUNICATIONS

Certificate. Designed to provide the background necessary to enter or advance in the field of software development.

Requirements: Computer literacy and associate-level math background.

Degree/Certificate Awarded: Postsecondary certificate.

Availability: Open to the public; national.

Primary Methods of Course Delivery and Response: Cable television; computer conferencing; electronic bulletin board; electronic mail; fax; public television; teleconferencing; telephone; videocassette.

For more information, contact: Chris Geith, Program and Market Developer, Distance Learning, Rochester Institute of Technology, P.O. Box 9887, Rochester, NY 14623; Telephone: 800-CALL-RIT; Fax: 716-475-5077; Internet: CMGODL@ritvax.isc.rit.edu; Bitnet: CMGODL@ritvax.

HEALTH SYSTEMS ADMINISTRATION

Certificate. Six-course sequence in health-care management and developing professional skills.

Requirements: Previous experience or course work in health care.

Degree/Certificate Awarded: Postsecondary certificate.

Availability: Open to the public; national.

Primary Methods of Course Delivery and Response: Cable television; computer conferencing; electronic bulletin board; electronic mail; fax; public television; teleconferencing; telephone; videocassette.

Accreditation: New York State Department of Education.

For more information, contact: Chris Geith, Program and Market Developer, Distance Learning, Rochester Institute of Technology, P.O. Box 9887, Rochester, NY 14623; Telephone: 800-CALL-RIT; Fax: 716-475-5077; Internet: CMGODL@ritvax.isc.rit.edu; Bitnet: CMGODL@ritvax.

SOLID WASTE MANAGEMENT TECHNOLOGY

Certificate. A 24-credit program covering applicability, design, construction, operation, and economics of major solid waste management technologies.

Requirements: Algebra; elementary statistics; two college sciences.

Degree/Certificate Awarded: Postsecondary certificate.

Availability: Open to the public; national.

Primary Methods of Course Delivery and Response: Cable television; computer conferencing; electronic bulletin board; electronic mail; fax; public television; teleconferencing; telephone; videocassette.

For more information, contact: Chris Geith, Program and Market Developer, Distance Learning, Rochester Institute of Technology, P.O. Box 9887, Rochester, NY 14623; Telephone: 800-CALL-RIT; Fax: 716-475-5077; Internet: CMGODL@ritvax.isc.rit.edu; Bitnet: CMGODL@ritvax.

EMERGENCY MANAGEMENT
Certificate. A five-course sequence designed for emergency professionals and aspiring professionals, including volunteer fire fighters, police officers, emergency medical workers, and industrial safety managers, as well as governmental and industrial emergency planners.

Requirements: None.

Degree/Certificate Awarded: Postsecondary certificate.

Availability: Open to the public; national.

Primary Methods of Course Delivery and Response: Cable television; computer conferencing; electronic bulletin board; electronic mail; fax; public television; teleconferencing; telephone; videocassette.

Accreditation: New York State Department of Education.

For more information, contact: Chris Geith, Program and Market Developer, Distance Learning, Rochester Institute of Technology, P.O. Box 9887, Rochester, NY 14623; Telephone: 800-CALL-RIT; Fax: 716-475-5077; Internet: CMGODL@ritvax.isc.rit.edu; Bitnet: CMGODL@ritvax.

APPLIED ARTS AND SCIENCE
B.S. in Applied Arts and Science. A multidisciplinary degree designed for students with an associate degree or equivalent.

Requirements: Matriculation not required for enrollment in individual courses.

Degree/Certificate Awarded: Bachelor's—B.S.

Availability: Open to the public and corporate subscribers; national.

Primary Methods of Course Delivery and Response: Audiographics; cable television; computer conferencing; electronic bulletin board; electronic mail; fax; public television; teleconferencing; telephone; videocassette.

For more information, contact: Chris Geith, Program and Market Developer, Distance Learning, Rochester Institute of Technology, P.O. Box 9887, Rochester, NY 14623; Telephone: 800-CALL-RIT; Fax: 716-475-5077; Internet: CMGODL@ritvax.isc.rit.edu; Bitnet: CMGODL@ritvax.

INDIVIDUAL COURSES
Rochester Institute of Technology offers individual for-credit courses in:

accounting (undergraduate); business/management (undergraduate); computer science (undergraduate and graduate); emergency management (undergraduate); environmental health and safety (undergraduate); health-care administration (undergraduate); information technology (undergraduate); liberal arts/general studies (undergraduate); telecommunications (undergraduate).

LAWRENCE D. PALUMBOS

Age: 39

Home: Rochester, New York

Institution: Rochester Institute of Technology

Courses taken: Via evening classes: principles of solid waste management, packaging and the environment, geology, recovery and conversion, hydrology. Via distance learning: recycling.

Academic achievement and goals: Palumbos holds a B.S. in business from RIT. He recently changed careers and is pursuing his B.S. in solid-waste management. The next distance learning course he will take is waste reduction.

"I was attending RIT full time and working part time with Monroe County's Recycling Hotline when I received a job offer from Waste Management, Inc., where I had previously worked as part of RIT's cooperative education program. So I switched to attending school part time and working full time.

"I took my first distance learning class, recycling, not by choice but because that was the only way it was offered. It turned out to exceed my expectations. I enjoyed not having to deal with driving and parking, and being able to view my professor at my leisure in the comfort of my air-conditioning when I was best suited to learn (i.e., when the gardening was done, the kids were in bed, and I had plenty of coffee).

"Instead of watching the late-night movie, I'd say to myself, 'Hey! I can watch that lecture again!' Since the study guide outlined what the professor was saying in the video, it was easy for me to index the content of each videotape. For example, if I wanted to repeat the part about municipal collection, I'd use the VCR counter and fast forward to that section of the lecture.

"My employer, Waste Management, Inc., supports continuing education for its employees. For one semester I was permitted to leave a little early twice a week to attend class. I also receive partial tuition reimbursement for successfully completed courses.

"As a person in sales, what is important to me about distance learning is that the college is serving me, the customer, by coming to me rather than always having me go to them. In addition to the time savings and flexibility, there are the energy savings to consider. With a class of 30, that's 30 fewer cars on the road, burning gas."

Palumbos is a customer service representative for Waste Management, Inc. In the 1970s he started his own construction business that emphasized energy efficiency in homes. In 1990 he sold his business to concentrate on his interest in the environment. He re-enrolled in RIT in 1991.

ROCKY MOUNTAIN COLLEGE
BILLINGS, MT 59102

Rocky Mountain College first offered a degree program via distance education in 1991.

Total enrollment in distance education programs (1992–93): 38.

Number graduating from distance programs (spring 1992): 3.

Rocky Mountain College offers an undergraduate degree at a distance comprised of its own courses and those offered through the Tribal College Consortium.

DEGREE PROGRAM

LIBERAL ARTS/GENERAL STUDIES
Rocky Mountain College/Tribal College Telecommunications Exchange. Includes upper-division general education, business, and education courses through Rocky Mountain College and Native American cultural courses through participants in the Tribal College Consortium.

Requirements: None.

Degree/Certificate Awarded: Bachelor's—B.A.

Consortium Affiliation: Tribal College Consortium, c/o Rocky Mountain College, Billings, Montana.

Availability: Open to the public; regional.

Primary Methods of Course Delivery and Response: Computer conferencing; telephone; videocassette.

On-Campus Component: One semester generally required.

For more information, contact: Richard Widmayer, Academic Vice President, Academic Affairs, Rocky Mountain College, Billings, MT 59102; Telephone: 406-657-1020; Fax: 406-259-9751.

INDIVIDUAL COURSES

Rocky Mountain College offers individual for-credit courses in: business/management (undergraduate); criminal justice/law (undergraduate); liberal arts/general studies (undergraduate); teacher education (undergraduate).

SAINT JOSEPH'S COLLEGE
WINDHAM, ME 04062-1198

Saint Joseph's College first offered a degree program via distance education in 1976.

Total enrollment in distance education programs (1992–93): 5,200.

Number graduating from distance programs (spring 1992): 369.

Distance programs at Saint Joseph's College are faculty directed, with an extensive support system to monitor and guide student progress. Programs have an extensive general education requirement in keeping with the institution's liberal arts base.

DEGREE PROGRAMS

HEALTH SERVICES ADMINISTRATION
Master's in Health Services Administration. An advanced program for health practitioners and managers seeking senior management positions in health-care settings.

Requirements: Bachelor's degree; two years health-care experience; prerequisite courses in statistics and health administration.

Degree/Certificate Awarded: Master's—M.H.S.A.

Availability: Open to the public; national.

Primary Methods of Course Delivery and Response: Fax; telephone.

On-Campus Component: Two-week summer residency.

Accreditation: New England Association of Schools and Colleges.

For more information, contact: Jamie Morin-Reynolds, Director, External Degree Program Admissions, Saint Joseph's College, Department 840, Windham, ME 04062-1198; Telephone: 207-892-7841; Fax: 207-892-7480.

HEALTH-CARE ADMINISTRATION
Bachelor of Science in Health-Care Administration Program. Professional education for students with prior clinical or technical training.

Requirements: High school diploma or GED; prior clinical or technical training.

Degree/Certificate Awarded: Bachelor's—B.S.H.C.A.

Availability: Open to the public; international.

Primary Methods of Course Delivery and Response: fax; telephone.

On-Campus Component: Three-week summer residency.

Accreditation: New England Association of Schools and Colleges.

For more information, contact: Jamie Morin-Reynolds, Director, External Degree Program Admissions, Saint Joseph's College, Department 840, Windham, ME 04062-1198; Telephone: 207-892-7841; Fax: 207-892-7480.

BUSINESS ADMINISTRATION

Bachelor of Science in Business Administration Program. Designed to increase adult students' theoretical and applied business knowledge.

Requirements: High school diploma or GED.

Degree/Certificate Awarded: Bachelor's—B.S.B.A.

Availability: Open to the public; international.

Primary Methods of Course Delivery and Response: Fax; telephone.

On-Campus Component: Three-week summer residency.

Accreditation: New England Association of Schools and Colleges.

For more information, contact: Jamie Morin-Reynolds, Director, External Degree Program Admissions, Saint Joseph's College, Department 840, Windham, ME 04062-1198; Telephone: 207-892-7841; Fax: 207-892-7480.

PROFESSIONAL ARTS

Bachelor of Science in Professional Arts. Designed as a degree completion program for individuals with license or certification in one of the health professions.

Requirements: High school diploma or GED; 30 SH credits or equivalent transfer credit.

Degree/Certificate Awarded: Bachelor's—B.S.P.A.

Availability: Open to the public; international.

Primary Methods of Course Delivery and Response: Fax; telephone.

On-Campus Component: Three-week summer residency.

Accreditation: New England Association of Schools and Colleges.

For more information, contact: Jamie Morin-Reynolds, Director, External Degree Program Admissions, Saint Joseph's College, Department 840, Windham, ME 04062-1198; Telephone: 207-892-7841; Fax: 207-892-7480.

RADIOLOGIC TECHNOLOGY

Bachelor of Science in Radiologic Technology. A post-certification program.

Requirements: Certificate or associate degree from an accredited program registered with ARRT; passing score on national registry exam.

Degree/Certificate Awarded: Bachelor's—B.S.R.T.

Availability: Open to the public; national.

Primary Methods of Course Delivery and Response: Fax; telephone.

On-Campus Component: Two-week summer residency.

Accreditation: New England Association of Schools and Colleges.

For more information, contact: Jamie Morin-Reynolds, Director, External Degree Program Admissions, Saint Joseph's College, Department 840, Windham, ME 04062-1198; Telephone: 207-892-7841; Fax: 207-892-7480.

HEALTH-CARE MANAGEMENT
Health-Care Management Certificate Program. Course work in health care management with concentrations in human resources, financial management, or general management.

Requirements: High school diploma or GED.

Degree/Certificate Awarded: Postsecondary certificate.

Availability: Open to the public; international.

Primary Methods of Course Delivery and Response: Fax; telephone; videocassette.

For more information, contact: Jamie Morin-Reynolds, Director, External Degree Program Admissions, Saint Joseph's College, Department 840, Windham, ME 04062-1198; Telephone: 207-892-7841; Fax: 207-892-7480.

HEALTH-CARE ADMINISTRATION
Long-Term Care Administration Certificate Program. Designed for long-term care administrators who do not wish to enroll in a bachelor's degree program. Can serve as refresher course and enable administrators to meet state licensing regulations or CE requirements.

Requirements: High school diploma or GED.

Degree/Certificate Awarded: Postsecondary certificate.

Availability: Open to the public; national.

Primary Methods of Course Delivery and Response: Fax; telephone.

Accreditation: New England Association of Schools and Colleges.

For more information, contact: Jamie Morin-Reynolds, Director, External Degree Program Admissions, Saint Joseph's College, Department 840, Windham, ME 04062-1198; Telephone: 207-892-7841; Fax: 207-892-7480.

LIBERAL STUDIES
Bachelor of Arts in Liberal Studies. An interdisciplinary program consisting of an integrated core curriculum and one or more interdisciplinary concentrations.

Requirements: High school diploma or GED.

Degree/Certificate Awarded: Bachelor's—B.A.L.S.

Availability: Open to the public; national.

Primary Methods of Course Delivery and Response: Audiocassette; fax; telephone.

On-Campus Component: Three-week summer residency.

For more information, contact: Jamie Morin-Reynolds, Director, External Degree Program Admissions, Saint Joseph's College, Department 840, Windham, ME 04062-1198; Telephone: 207-892-7841; Fax: 207-892-7480.

BUSINESS ADMINISTRATION
Business Administration Certificate Program. Offers a solid background in business administration theory and applications with tracks in management and marketing.

Requirements: High school diploma or GED.

Degree/Certificate Awarded: Postsecondary certificate.

Availability: Open to the public; international.

Primary Methods of Course Delivery and Response: Fax; telephone.

Accreditation: New England Association of Schools and Colleges.

For more information, contact: Jamie Morin-Reynolds, Director, External Degree Program Admissions, Saint Joseph's College, Department 840, Windham, ME 04062-1198; Telephone: 207-892-7841; Fax: 207-892-7480.

INDIVIDUAL COURSES

Saint Joseph's College offers individual for-credit courses in: business/management (undergraduate); health-care administration (undergraduate and graduate); liberal arts/general studies (undergraduate); long-term care administration (undergraduate).

SAINT MARY'S COLLEGE OF MINNESOTA
WINONA, MN 55987-1399

Saint Mary's College of Minnesota first offered a degree program via distance education in 1993.

The IDEAL Institute of Saint Mary's College of Minnesota provides distance learning opportunities to rural areas of Minnesota.

DEGREE PROGRAM

DISTANCE LEARNING
The Effective Use of Distance Learning. Focuses on humanizing the distance learning environment.

Requirements: None.

Degree/Certificate Awarded: Postsecondary certificate.

Availability: Open to the public; statewide.

Primary Methods of Course Delivery and Response: Compressed-video television; videoconferencing.

For more information, contact: Harry Hurley, Director, IDEAL Institute, 8100 34th Ave. S, Bloomington, MN 55425; Telephone: 612-853-5686; Fax: 612-853-4409.

INDIVIDUAL COURSES

Saint Mary's College of Minnesota offers individual for-credit courses in: computer science (undergraduate); criminal justice/law (undergraduate); teacher education (undergraduate).

SALVE REGINA UNIVERSITY
NEWPORT, RI 02840-4192

Salve Regina University first offered a degree program via distance education in 1985.

Total enrollment in distance education programs (1992–93): 225.

Number graduating from distance programs (spring 1992): 14.

Courses offered through extension study at Salve Regina University are prepared by faculty members to provide a structured, step-by-step approach to learning while allowing students flexibility in time and place of study. The process involves a one-on-one relationship with instructors, who guide learning and monitor students' progress by means of written comments and technological communication. Graduate students may complete a master's degree through regular on-campus courses, extension courses, or a combination.

DEGREE PROGRAM

CORRECTIONAL ADMINISTRATION
Correction studies, management, and humanities courses designed to meet the needs of middle-management corrections personnel.

Requirements: Bachelor's degree; MAT or GRE.

Degree/Certificate Awarded: Master's—M.I.T.

Availability: Open to the public; national.

Primary Methods of Course Delivery and Response: Fax; telephone.

On-Campus Component: Two weeks.

For more information, contact: Graduate Admissions, Salve Regina University, Newport, RI 02840; Telephone: 800-321-7124; Fax: 401-847-0372.

INDIVIDUAL COURSES

Salve Regina University offers individual for-credit courses in: accounting (graduate); business/management (graduate); criminal justice/law (graduate); international relations (graduate); liberal arts/general studies (graduate).

SAN JOSE STATE UNIVERSITY
SAN JOSE, CA 95192-0169

San Jose State University first offered a degree program via distance education in 1986.
Total enrollment in distance education programs (1992–93): 450.

Number graduating from distance programs (spring 1992): 35.

The Television Education Network (TEN), an outreach program developed by San Jose State University's Office of Continuing Education, is a four-channel TV broadcast network, in color, with interactive audio. Regular campus classes and special programs are transmitted live from two on-campus studio classrooms to remote classrooms at industries, companies, community colleges, and designated K–12 school receive sites.

DEGREE PROGRAMS

SPECIAL EDUCATION
Credential—Special Education for Learning Handicapped. Designed to give beginning and experienced teachers a broader base of knowledge and competency for meeting special educational needs of individuals with learning handicaps.

Requirements: Valid California Basic Teaching credential.

Degree/Certificate Awarded: Postsecondary certificate.

Availability: Open to the public; local.

Primary Methods of Course Delivery and Response: Closed-circuit television; ITFS.

On-Campus Component: Two courses (one semester).

For more information, contact: Ted Montemurro, Division Head, Special Education, San Jose State University, Sweeney Hall 204, San Jose, CA 95192-0169; Telephone: 408-924-3700.

MANAGEMENT
Total Quality Management Certificate Program. Focus is on the practical aspects of TQM that translate directly into improved quality and enhanced productivity and service.

Degree/Certificate Awarded: Postsecondary certificate.

Availability: Open to the public; local.

Primary Methods of Course Delivery and Response: Closed-circuit television; ITFS.

For more information, contact: Dr. Elizabeth Perrin, Associate Director, TQM, Continuing Education, San Jose State University, One Washington Square, IRC 213A, San Jose, CA 95120; Telephone: 408-924-2859; Fax: 408-924-2881.

INDIVIDUAL COURSES

San Jose State University offers individual for-credit courses in: accounting (undergraduate); business/management (undergraduate); environmental health and safety (undergraduate); liberal arts/general studies (undergraduate); teacher education (undergraduate and graduate).

SOUTHERN METHODIST UNIVERSITY
DALLAS, TX 75275

Southern Methodist University first offered a degree program via distance education in 1967.

_____

The School of Engineering and Applied Science offers distance-education graduate programs via three delivery systems: the TAGER television network (a service of the Alliance for Higher Education), the National Technological University (NTU) satellite system, and videotape. Part-time students can view and complete graduate-level courses at their workplace. On-site education allows students to attend classes with co-workers and better appreciate the relevance of course work to the work environment.

DEGREE PROGRAMS

ENGINEERING MANAGEMENT
Master's in Engineering Management.

Requirements: Same as for on-campus graduate students.

Degree/Certificate Awarded: Master's—M.S.

Consortium Affiliation: Alliance for Higher Education, 17103 Preston Rd., Lock Box 107, Suite 250, Dallas, TX 75248-373.

Availability: Open to the public; North Texas area only.

Primary Methods of Course Delivery and Response: Satellite television; two-way audio.

On-Campus Component: Exams usually given on Southern Methodist University campus.

For more information, contact: James G. Dunham, Assistant Dean of Graduate Studies, School of Engineering and Applied Science, Southern Methodist University, Dallas, TX 75275; Telephone: 214-768-3051; Fax: 214-768-4138.

OPERATIONS RESEARCH
Master's in Operations Research.

Requirements: Same as for on-campus graduate students.

Degree/Certificate Awarded: Master's—M.S.

Consortium Affiliation: Alliance for Higher Education, 17103 Preston Rd., Lock Box 107, Suite 250, Dallas, TX 75248-373.

Availability: Open to the public; North Texas area only.

Primary Methods of Course Delivery and Response: Satellite television; two-way audio.

On-Campus Component: Exams usually given on Southern Methodist University campus.

For more information, contact: James G. Dunham, Assistant Dean of Graduate

Studies, School of Engineering and Applied Science, Southern Methodist University, Dallas, TX 75275; Telephone: 214-768-3051; Fax: 214-768-4138.

COMPUTER ENGINEERING
Master's in Computer Engineering.

Requirements: Same as for on-campus graduate students.

Degree/Certificate Awarded: Master's—M.S.

Consortium Affiliation: Alliance for Higher Education, 17103 Preston Rd., Lock Box 107, Suite 250, Dallas, TX 75248-373.

Availability: Open to the public; North Texas area only.

Primary Methods of Course Delivery and Response: Satellite television; two-way audio.

On-Campus Component: Exams usually given on Southern Methodist University campus.

For more information, contact: James G. Dunham, Assistant Dean of Graduate Studies, School of Engineering and Applied Science, Southern Methodist University, Dallas, TX 75275; Telephone: 214-768-3051; Fax: 214-768-4138.

COMPUTER SCIENCE
Master's in Computer Science.

Requirements: Same as for on-campus students.

Degree/Certificate Awarded: Master's—M.S.

Consortium Affiliation: Alliance for Higher Education, 17103 Preston Rd., Lock Box 107, Suite 250, Dallas, TX 75248-373.

Availability: Open to the public; North Texas area only.

Primary Methods of Course Delivery and Response: Satellite television; two-way audio.

On-Campus Component: Exams usually given on Southern Methodist University campus.

For more information, contact: James G. Dunham, Assistant Dean of Graduate Studies, School of Engineering and Applied Science, Southern Methodist University, Dallas, TX 75275; Telephone: 214-768-3051; Fax: 214-768-4138.

MECHANICAL ENGINEERING
Master's in Mechanical Engineering.

Requirements: Same as for on-campus graduate students.

Degree/Certificate Awarded: Master's—M.S.

Consortium Affiliation: Alliance for Higher Education, 17103 Preston Rd., Lock Box 107, Suite 250, Dallas, TX 75248-373.

Availability: Open to the public; North Texas area only.

Primary Methods of Course Delivery and Response: Satellite television; two-way audio.

On-Campus Component: Exams usually given on Southern Methodist University campus.

For more information, contact: James G. Dunham, Assistant Dean of Graduate

Studies, School of Engineering and Applied Science, Southern Methodist University, Dallas, TX 75275; Telephone: 214-768-3051; Fax: 214-768-4138.

ELECTRICAL ENGINEERING
Master's in Electrical Engineering.

Requirements: Same as for on-campus graduate students.

Degree/Certificate Awarded: Master's—M.S.

Consortium Affiliation: Alliance for Higher Education, 17103 Preston Rd., Lock Box 107, Suite 250, Dallas, TX 75248-373.

Availability: Open to the public; North Texas area only.

Primary Methods of Course Delivery and Response: Satellite television; two-way audio.

On-Campus Component: Exams usually given on Southern Methodist University campus.

For more information, contact: James G. Dunham, Assistant Dean of Graduate Studies, School of Engineering and Applied Science, Southern Methodist University, Dallas, TX 75275; Telephone: 214-768-3051; Fax: 214-768-4138.

ENGINEERING
National Technological University Engineering Master's Programs.

Requirements: Same as for on-campus graduate students.

Degree/Certificate Awarded: Master's—M.S.

Availability: Open to the public; national.

Primary Methods of Course Delivery and Response: Computer conferencing; electronic mail; fax; satellite television; telephone.

Accreditation: Commission on Institutions of Higher Education of the North Central Association of Colleges and Schools.

For more information, contact: James G. Dunham, Assistant Dean of Graduate Studies, School of Engineering and Applied Science, Southern Methodist University, Dallas, TX 75275; Telephone: 214-768-3051; Fax: 214-768-4138.

INDIVIDUAL COURSES

Southern Methodist University offers individual for-credit courses in: computer science (graduate); engineering (graduate).

SOUTHERN OREGON STATE COLLEGE
ASHLAND, OR 97520

Southern Oregon State College first offered a degree program via distance education in 1992.
Total enrollment in distance education programs (1992–93): 100.

———————

Southern Oregon State College employs Oregon ED-NETS Networks I, II, and III to deliver programs in business, education, and nursing to southwestern Oregon.

DEGREE PROGRAM

EDUCATION
M.S. in Education. Core courses in elementary and secondary education.

Requirements: Bachelor's degree; GRE; basic teacher certification.

Degree/Certificate Awarded: Master's—M.S.

Availability: Open to certified teachers; regional.

Primary Methods of Course Delivery and Response: Compressed-video television; computer conferencing; fax; telephone; videocassette.

On-Campus Component: Orientation and some weekend college courses or summer session.

Accreditation: Oregon Council for Accreditation of Teacher Education, National Council for Accreditation of Teacher Education, Northwest Assocation of Schools and Colleges.

For more information, contact: David Hoffman, Graduate Coordinator, Department of Education, Southern Oregon State College, Ashland, OR 97520; Telephone: 503-552-6283.

INDIVIDUAL COURSES

Southern Oregon State College offers individual for-credit courses in: business/management (undergraduate and graduate); liberal arts/general studies (undergraduate and graduate); nursing (undergraduate); teacher education (graduate).

Southwestern Assemblies of God College
Waxahachie, TX 75165

Southwestern Assemblies of God College first offered a degree program via distance education in 1984.

Total enrollment in distance education programs (1992–93): 546.

Number graduating from distance programs (spring 1992): 37.

The distance education program at Southwestern Assemblies of God College offers resident credit and credit for experiential learning; financial aid and scholarships; toll-free access to professors; and full graduation participation.

DEGREE PROGRAM

ADULT AND CONTINUING EDUCATION

Campus-based external adult degree program. Includes general education core and 15 specializations.

Requirements: Statement of Christian faith.

Degree/Certificate Awarded: Bachelor's—B.C.A.

Availability: Open to those who make a statement of Christian faith; national.

Primary Methods of Course Delivery and Response: Audiocassette; computer conferencing; teleconferencing; telephone; videocassette.

On-Campus Component: Two days for registration at beginning of each semester.

Accreditation: Southern Association of Colleges and Schools.

For more information, contact: Jim Jessup, Director, Adult and Continuing Education, Southwestern Assemblies of God College, 1200 Sycamore, Waxahachie, TX 75165; Telephone: 214-937-4010; Fax: 214-923-0488.

INDIVIDUAL COURSES

Southwestern Assemblies of God College offers individual for-credit courses in: accounting (undergraduate); business/management (undergraduate); computer science (undergraduate); liberal arts/general studies (undergraduate); teacher education (undergraduate).

STANFORD UNIVERSITY
STANFORD, CA 94305

Stanford University first offered a degree program via distance education in 1968. Total enrollment in distance education programs (1992–93): 3352.

The distance education program run by the Stanford Instructional Television Network (SITN) for the School of Engineering offers live broadcast of courses being held on campus (250 classes each year) to over 160 different industry and government locations in the San Francisco Bay area. Most broadcast classes are in electrical engineering and computer science. Although they are not encouraged to do so, it is possible for students in these degree programs to take all required courses through television. Other degree programs, such as mechanical engineering, aeronautics and astronautics, engineering-economic systems, industrial engineering, and engineering management, are open to distance education students from industry, but it is likely they will attend a large number of their required classes on campus.

DEGREE PROGRAMS

COMPUTER SCIENCE
Master's degree or certificate program.

Degree/Certificate Awarded: Master's—M.S., postsecondary certificate.

Availability: Open to corporate and government subscribers; San Francisco Bay area.

Primary Methods of Course Delivery and Response: Closed-circuit television; compressed-video television; ITFS Microwave delivery system; videoconferencing.

On-Campus Component: One quarter residency for students outside live broadcast area (San Francisco Bay area).

For more information, contact: Carolyn Schultz, Associate Director, School of Engineering, SITN, 401 Durand, Stanford, CA, 94305-4036; Telephone: 415-725-3000; Fax: 415-725-3000; Internet: CSchultz@leland.Stanford.edu.

ELECTRICAL ENGINEERING
Master's degree or certificate program.

Degree/Certificate Awarded: Master's—M.S., postsecondary certificate.

Availability: Open to corporate and government subscribers; San Francisco Bay area.

Primary Methods of Course Delivery and Response: Closed-circuit television; compressed-video television; ITFS microwave delivery system; videoconferencing.

On-Campus Component: One quarter residency for students outside of live broadcast area (San Francisco Bay area).

For more information, contact: Carolyn Schultz, Associate Director, School of

Engineering, SITN, 401 Durand, Stanford, CA, 94305-4036; Telephone: 415-725-3000; Fax: 415-725-3000; Internet: CSchultz@leland.Stanford.edu.

INDIVIDUAL COURSES

Stanford University offers individual for-credit courses in: computer science (undergraduate and graduate); engineering (undergraduate and graduate).

STATE UNIVERSITY OF NEW YORK, EMPIRE STATE COLLEGE

SARATOGA SPRINGS, NY 12866-4391

The State University of New York, Empire State College, first offered a degree program via distance education in 1979.

Total enrollment in distance education programs (1992–93): 1,300.

Number graduating from distance programs (spring 1992): 80.

The Center for Distance Learning offers associate and bachelor's degree programs and individual courses in business, human services, and interdisciplinary studies using various technologies, including computer, satellite, and telephone. These programs are individually designed by each student working with a faculty adviser to respond to students' circumstances, needs, and experience. Students can often apply credit earned from previous college study toward their degree programs, and credit can be earned through approved testing programs such as CLEP.

DEGREE PROGRAMS

BUSINESS
Bachelor of Science in Business.

Degree/Certificate Awarded: Bachelor's—B.S., B.P.S.

Availability: Open to the public; national.

Primary Methods of Course Delivery and Response: Audiocassette; computer conferencing; electronic mail; satellite television; telephone; videocassette.

For more information, contact: Daniel Granger, Director, Center for Distance Learning, Empire State College, Saratoga Springs, NY 12866; Telephone: 518-587-2100; Fax: 518-587-5404; Bitnet: CDL@SNYESCVA.

HUMAN SERVICES
Bachelor's Degree in Human Services.

Degree/Certificate Awarded: Bachelor's—B.A., B.S., B.P.S.

Availability: Open to the public; national.

Primary Methods of Course Delivery and Response: Audiocassette; computer conferencing; electronic mail; satellite television; telephone; videocassette.

For more information, contact: Daniel Granger, Director, Center for Distance Learning, Empire State College, Saratoga Springs, NY 12866; Telephone: 518-587-2100; Fax: 518-587-5404; Bitnet: CDL@SNYESCVA.

INTERDISCIPLINARY STUDIES
Bachelor's Degree in Interdisciplinary Studies.

Degree/Certificate Awarded: Bachelor's—B.A., B.S.

Availability: Open to the public; national.

Primary Methods of Course Delivery and Response: Audiocassette; computer conferencing; electronic mail; satellite television; telephone; videocassette.

For more information, contact: Daniel Granger, Director, Center for Distance Learning, Empire State College, Saratoga Springs, NY 12866; Telephone: 518-587-2100; Fax: 518-587-5404; Bitnet: CDL@SNYESCVA.

INDIVIDUAL COURSES

The State University of New York, Empire State College, offers individual for-credit courses in: accounting (undergraduate); business/management (undergraduate); human services (undergraduate); liberal arts/general studies (undergraduate).

SYRACUSE UNIVERSITY
SYRACUSE, NY 13244

Syracuse University first offered a degree program via distance education in 1966.

Syracuse University's programs are conducted on a limited residency model, with short, intensive on-campus residence periods followed by longer periods of home study.

DEGREE PROGRAMS

CRIMINAL JUSTICE
Bachelor of Science in Criminal Justice. A 120-credit major with significant liberal arts courses.

Requirements: Letters of recommendation; 2.0 GPA for transfer students.

Degree/Certificate Awarded: Bachelor's—B.S.

Availability: Open to the public; international.

Primary Methods of Course Delivery and Response: Fax; telephone.

On-Campus Component: One week each semester.

For more information, contact: Robert Colley, Director, Independent Study Degree Programs, Syracuse University, 610 East Fayette St., Syracuse, NY 13244; Telephone: 315-443-3284; Fax: 315-443-1928; Bitnet: RM COLLEY@SUADMIN.BITNET.

BUSINESS ADMINISTRATION
Bachelor of Science in Business Administration. A 120-credit general business administration degree.

Requirements: Letters of recommendation; 2.5 GPA for transfer students.

Degree/Certificate Awarded: Bachelor's—B.S.

Availability: Open to the public; international.

Primary Methods of Course Delivery and Response: Fax; telephone.

On-Campus Component: One week each semester.

Accreditation: American Assembly of Collegiate Schools of Business.

For more information, contact: Robert Colley, Director, Independent Study Degree Programs, Syracuse University, 610 East Fayette St., Syracuse, NY 13244; Telephone: 315-443-3284; Fax: 315-443-1928; Bitnet: RM COLLEY@SUADMIN.BITNET.

RESTAURANT AND FOOD SERVICE MANAGEMENT
Bachelor of Science in Restaurant and Food Service Management. A 124-credit bachelor's degree covering management in all areas of the food service industry.

Requirements: Letters of recommendation; 2.0 GPA for transfer students.

Degree/Certificate Awarded: Bachelor's—B.S.

THE ELECTRONIC UNIVERSITY

Availability: Open to the public; international.

Primary Methods of Course Delivery and Response: Fax; telephone.

On-Campus Component: One week each semester.

For more information, contact: Robert Colley, Director, Independent Study Degree Programs, Syracuse University, 610 East Fayette St., Syracuse, NY 13244; Telephone: 315-443-3284; Fax: 315-443-1928; Bitnet: RM COLLEY@SUADMIN.BITNET.

LIBERAL STUDIES
Bachelor of Arts in Liberal Studies. A 120-credit program with group requirements in liberal arts.

Requirements: Letters of recommendation; 2.0 GPA for transfer students.

Degree/Certificate Awarded: Bachelor's—B.A.

Availability: Open to the public; international.

Primary Methods of Course Delivery and Response: Fax; telephone.

On-Campus Component: One week each semester.

For more information, contact: Robert Colley, Director, Independent Study Degree Programs, Syracuse University, 610 East Fayette St., Syracuse, NY 13244; Telephone: 315-443-3284; Fax: 315-443-1928; Bitnet: RM COLLEY@SUADMIN.BITNET.

ILLUSTRATION/ADVERTISING DESIGN
Master of Arts in Illustration or Advertising Design. A 30-credit mid-career program for professionals with significant experience in advertising or graphic design or illustration.

Requirements: Bachelor's degree; portfolio; letters of recommendation.

Degree/Certificate Awarded: Master's—M.A.

Availability: Open to working professionals in illustration or design; international.

Primary Methods of Course Delivery and Response: Fax; telephone.

On-Campus Component: Four weeks per year over two years.

Accreditation: National Association of Schools of Art and Design.

For more information, contact: Robert Colley, Director, Independent Study Degree Programs, Syracuse University, 610 East Fayette St., Syracuse, NY 13244; Telephone: 315-443-3284; Fax: 315-443-1928; Bitnet: RM COLLEY@SUADMIN.BITNET.

BUSINESS ADMINISTRATION
Master's in Business Administration. A 54-credit general M.B.A.—39 core credits and 15 elective credits.

Requirements: Bachelor's degree; two letters of recommendation; three years professional experience.

Degree/Certificate Awarded: Master's—M.B.A.

Availability: Open to the public; international.

Primary Methods of Course Delivery and Response: Fax; telephone.

On-Campus Component: One week each semester.

Accreditation: American Assembly of Collegiate Schools of Business.

For more information, contact: Robert Colley, Director, Independent Study Degree Programs, Syracuse University, 610 East Fayette St., Syracuse, NY 13244; Telephone: 315-443-3284; Fax: 315-443-1928; Bitnet: RM COLLEY@SUADMIN.BITNET.

NURSING

Master's in Nursing. Curriculum emphasizes management skills with a clinical specialization.

Requirements: B.S. in nursing; GRE; letters of recommendation.

Degree/Certificate Awarded: Master's—M.Nurs.

Availability: Open to the public; international.

Primary Methods of Course Delivery and Response: Electronic mail; fax; interactive videodisc; telephone.

On-Campus Component: Nine weeks over four summers.

Accreditation: National League for Nursing.

For more information, contact: Robert Colley, Director, Independent Study Degree Programs, Syracuse University, 610 East Fayette St., Syracuse, NY 13244; Telephone: 315-443-3284; Fax: 315-443-1928; Bitnet: RM COLLEY@SUADMIN.BITNET.

SOCIAL SCIENCE

Master of Social Science. Two-year, 30-credit degree program emphasizing international relations.

Requirements: Bachelor's degree; letters of recommendation.

Degree/Certificate Awarded: Master's—M.S.Sc.

Availability: Open to the public; international.

Primary Methods of Course Delivery and Response: Fax; telephone.

On-Campus Component: Two weeks each summer for two summers.

For more information, contact: Robert Colley, Director, Independent Study Degree Programs, Syracuse University, 610 East Fayette St., Syracuse, NY 13244; Telephone: 315-443-3284; Fax: 315-443-1928; Bitnet: RM COLLEY@SUADMIN.BITNET.

LIBRARY SCIENCE

Master of Library Science. Strategic management of information resources, library science, communications, information science, computer science, business, and public policy.

Requirements: 3.0 GPA; combined verbal and quantitative score of 1000 on GRE; 550 TOEFL.

Degree/Certificate Awarded: Master's—M.L.S.

Availability: Open to the public; international.

Primary Methods of Course Delivery and Response: Fax; telephone.

On-Campus Component: Three two-week summer sessions, plus an additional one-week residency session.

Accreditation: American Library Association.

For more information, contact: Robert Colley, Director, Independent Study Degree Programs, Syracuse University, 610 East Fayette St., Syracuse, NY 13244; Telephone: 315-443-3284; Fax: 315-443-1928; Bitnet: RM COLLEY@SUADMIN.BITNET.

INDIVIDUAL COURSES

Syracuse University offers individual for-credit courses in: criminal justice/law (undergraduate); food service management (undergraduate); liberal arts/general studies (undergraduate).

TEXAS TECH UNIVERSITY
LUBBOCK, TX 79409

Texas Tech University first offered a degree program via distance education in 1991.
Total enrollment in distance education programs (1992–93): 280.

Texas Tech University offers graduate courses in education over Tech Link, a compressed-video system. A general master's degree program in engineering is offered via videotape.

DEGREE PROGRAMS

EDUCATION
Tech Link. Selected courses in higher education, educational technology, and educational psychology.

Requirements: Same as for on-campus graduate students.

Degree/Certificate Awarded: Master's—M.Ed., doctorate—D.Ed., postsecondary certificate.

Availability: Open to the public in Lubbock, Amarillo, Odessa, and El Paso, TX.

Primary Method of Course Delivery and Response: Compressed-video television; videotape.

On-Campus Component: Must complete residency requirement for the D.Ed. A complete master's or doctoral program in education is not available via Tech Link.

For more information, contact: Michael Mezack III, Director, Continuing Education, Texas Tech University, Box 42191, Lubbock, TX 79409; Telephone: 806-742-3797; Fax: 806-742-2318.

ENGINEERING
Undifferentiated Master of Engineering.

Requirements: Undergraduate degree in engineering; other requirements same as those for on-campus students.

Degree/Certification Awarded: Master's—M.E.

Availability: Open to the public; West Texas area only.

Primary Method of Course Delivery and Response: Videocassette.

For more information, contact: Dr. Carla Relaford, ITV Director, KTXT-TV, Texas Tech University, Box 42161, Lubbock, TX 79409; Telephone: 806-742-2209; Fax: 806-742-1274.

INDIVIDUAL COURSES

Texas Tech University offers individual for-credit courses in: higher education (graduate); teacher education (graduate).

WILLIAM RUTHERFORD

Age: 39

Home: Odessa, Texas

Institution: Texas Tech University

Courses taken: Three classes via a Texas Tech instructor who came to the Odessa site: critical issues in higher education, readings in higher education, advanced seminar in higher education; one class in Odessa via Techlink interactive television: development and finance; plus a two-semester residency that required on-site attendance at the Lubbock campus.

Academic goals: To obtain an Ed.D. in higher education by completing 15 remaining hours plus a dissertation.

"I work full time at a community college that is 140 miles away from the Texas Tech campus in Lubbock. At first I was skeptical; I wasn't sure that the classes conducted by interactive TV would be as good as having the instructor in the classroom. But I can honestly say that they were just as good. We could ask questions and interact with people at all four sites. We had two monitors and could see two of the other three sites at all times. If I wanted to ask a question of someone at the Amarillo site and it was not showing up on the monitor, the teacher would just punch a button to bring it up. We could see and hear everything clearly—even papers rustling. Literally the only thing you could not do was `reach out and touch' them.

"In fact, in some ways it was better than being on-site. For example, we simply created

[visual aids] on regular-size sheets of paper and fed them into what amounted to a high-tech overhead projector. It could even zoom in on tiny paragraphs on a book page to enlarge them on the video screen so everyone could read them.

"Distance learning is the only practical way I can keep up with my professional career education. When I commuted those two semesters to Lubbock, I didn't get in until midnight and then had to be up at 7 A.M. to teach school. Distance learning has enabled me to spend more time with my wife and children. It's not just the wave of the future—it's already here."

Rutherford serves on the faculty of Odessa College, where he teaches social sciences.

THOMAS EDISON STATE COLLEGE
TRENTON, NJ 08608-1176

Thomas Edison State College first offered a degree program via distance education in 1972.

Total enrollment in distance education programs (1992–93): 10,000.

Number graduating from distance programs (spring 1992): 799.

The Guided Study Program at the Center for Directed Independent Adult Learning offers 50 courses that can be taken individually or applied toward a bachelor's degree.

DEGREE PROGRAM

LIBERAL ARTS/GENERAL STUDIES
Guided Study. Distance courses for adults in the humanities, social sciences, business, and natural sciences.

Requirements: None.

Degree/Certificate Awarded: Bachelor's—B.A.

Availability: Open to the public; national.

Primary Methods of Course Delivery and Response: Audiocassette; computer conferencing; electronic mail; telephone; videocassette.

For more information, contact: Thomas Edison State College, DIAL, 101 West State St., Trenton, NJ 08608-1176; Telephone: 609-292-6317; Fax: 609-984-8447.

INDIVIDUAL COURSES

Thomas Edison State College offers individual for-credit courses in: business/management (undergraduate); computer science (undergraduate); foreign languages (undergraduate); liberal arts/general studies (undergraduate).

UNIVERSITY OF ALABAMA
TUSCALOOSA, AL 35487-0388

The University of Alabama first offered a degree program via distance education in 1992.
Total enrollment in distance education programs (1992–93): 170.

The University of Alabama's Office of Educational Telecommunications houses two distance education programs. The Quality Extended Site Telecourses (QUEST) program provides credit and noncredit courses on videotape. On-campus classes are taped as they occur and are shipped to established sites where students gather to take the classes via videotape. Each site has a coordinator who provides handouts and proctors examinations. Graduate courses are offered in engineering and business, and a master's degree in aerospace engineering is available. Undergraduate courses are offered in engineering, business, and nursing. The Intercampus Interactive Telecommunications System (IITS) connects the three campuses in the University of Alabama System—Tuscaloosa, Birmingham, and Huntsville—in live, interactive teleconferencing. The system extends the resources of the three campuses and provides programs not available at each university. For example, the University of Alabama offers Master of Library Studies and Master of Advertising and Public Relations degrees; students can enroll in these courses at Tuscaloosa, Birmingham, or Huntsville. Four additional sites are planned.

DEGREE PROGRAMS

AEROSPACE ENGINEERING
Quality University Extended Site Telecourses (QUEST). Master of Aerospace Engineering degree available via videotape. QUEST also offers other credit courses on videotape at graduate and undergraduate levels.

Requirements: B.S. in engineering or related field; B average for last 60 hours; B.S. from Accreditation Board for Engineering and Technology–accredited institution or 1500 cumulative GRE. For other QUEST courses, regular admission requirements.

Degree/Certificate Awarded: Master's—M.S.A.E.

Availability: Open to the public; national.

Primary Method of Course Delivery and Response: Videocassette.

Accreditation: Accreditation Board for Engineering and Technology.

ADVERTISING AND PUBLIC RELATIONS
Master of Advertising and Public Relations.

Requirements: Same as for on-campus students.

Degree/Certificate Awarded: Master's—M.S.

Availability: Open to the public; national.

Primary Methods of Course Delivery and Response: Compressed-video television; fax.

Accreditation: Accrediting Council of Education in Journalism and Mass Communication.

For more information, contact: Carroll Tingle, Director, Educational Telecommunications, University of Alabama, Box 870388, Tuscaloosa, AL 35487-0388; Telephone: 205-348-9278; Fax: 205-348-9246; Internet: CTINGLE@UAIVM.UA.EDU.

LIBRARY SCIENCE
Master of Library Studies.

Requirements: Same as for on-campus students.

Degree/Certificate Awarded: Master's—M.L.S.

Availability: Open to the public; statewide as well as to out-of-state sites with compatible compressed-video equipment.

Primary Methods of Course Delivery and Response: Compressed-video television; fax.

Accreditation: American Library Association.

For more information, contact: Carroll Tingle, Director, Educational Telecommunications, University of Alabama, Box 870388, Tuscaloosa, AL 35487-0388; Telephone: 205-348-9278; Fax: 205-348-9246; Internet: CTINGLE@UAIVM.UA.EDU.

INDIVIDUAL COURSES

The University of Alabama offers individual for-credit courses in: business/management (graduate); communications (graduate); computer science (undergraduate and graduate); engineering (undergraduate and graduate); nursing (undergraduate).

UNIVERSITY OF ALASKA, FAIRBANKS
FAIRBANKS, AK 99775-0885

The University of Alaska, Fairbanks, first offered a degree program via distance education in 1970.

Total enrollment in distance education programs (1992–93): 2,600.

Number graduating from distance programs (spring 1992): 11.

The University of Alaska, Fairbanks, has a long history of bringing postsecondary education to rural citizens, particularly Alaska natives, through distance delivery of courses and programs. Delivery takes place primarily through audio conferencing, mail, fax, and computer, but audiographics, broadcast video, and compressed video are also used experimentally. Faculty and administrative support services are decentralized and located in various regional campuses and centers.

DEGREE PROGRAMS

EDUCATION
Cross-Cultural Education Development Program (X-CED). Courses leading to a B.Ed. and elementary or secondary school certification.

Requirements: 45 credits completed; 2.5 GPA; demonstrated academic ability; evidence of long-term commitment to the Alaska region; familiarity with native language and culture; interest and potential for success in the field.

Degree/Certificate Awarded: Bachelor's—B.Ed.

Availability: Open to rural Alaska residents, north and west of the Alaska Range.

Primary Methods of Course Delivery and Response: Audiocassette; electronic mail; fax; teleconferencing; telephone; videocassette.

Accreditation: National Council for Accreditation of Teacher Education.

For more information, contact: Ray Barnhardt, Coordinator, Off-Campus Programs, School of Education, University of Alaska, Fairbanks, 706 C Gruening Bldg., Fairbanks, AK 99775; Telephone: 907-474-6431; Fax: 907-474-5451; Bitnet: FFRJB @ Alaska.

EDUCATION
Master of Education. Four areas of specialization: cross-cultural education, curriculum and instruction, language and literacy, and educational leadership.

Requirements: Bachelor's degree with 24 credits in education; 3.0 GPA; one year teaching experience.

Degree/Certificate Awarded: Master's—M.Ed.

Availability: Open to rural Alaska residents; statewide.

Primary Methods of Course Delivery and Response: Audiocassette; electronic mail; fax; teleconferencing; telephone; videocassette.

On-Campus Component: At least 15 of the 36 required credits.

Accreditation: National Council for Accreditation of Teacher Education.

For more information, contact: Ray Barnhardt, Coordinator, Off-Campus Programs, School of Education, University of Alaska, Fairbanks, 706 C Gruening Bldg., Fairbanks, AK 99775; Telephone: 907-474-6431; Fax: 907-474-5451; Bitnet: FFRJB @ Alaska.

RURAL DEVELOPMENT
Degree completion program. Addresses rural/community issues and concerns such as land resources, local government, and small business management.

Requirements: 45 credits completed; 2.5 GPA.

Degree/Certificate Awarded: Bachelor's—B.A.

Availability: Open to rural Alaska residents north and west of the Alaska Range.

Primary Methods of Course Delivery and Response: Audiocassette; electronic mail; fax; teleconferencing; telephone; videocassette.

For more information, contact: Pat Dubbs, Department Head, Rural Development, University of Alaska, Fairbanks, 707 B Gruening Bldg., Fairbanks, AK 99775; Telephone: 907-474-6432; Fax: 907-474-5451; Bitnet: FFPJD @ Alaska.

SOCIAL WORK
Degree completion program. Within the framework of behavioral sciences, concentrates on emotional and social problems of individuals, families, and communities.

Requirements: 45 credits completed; 2.5 GPA.

Degree/Certificate Awarded: Bachelor's—B.A.

Availability: Open to rural Alaska residents north and west of the Alaskan Range.

Primary Methods of Course Delivery and Response: Audiocassette; electronic mail; fax; teleconferencing; telephone; videocassette.

Accreditation: Council on Social Work Education.

For more information, contact: Gerald Berman, Department Head, Behavioral Sciences and Human Services, University of Alaska, Fairbanks, 702 B Gruening Bldg., Fairbanks, AK 99775; Telephone: 907-474-6516; Fax: 907-474-5451; Bitnet: FFGSB @ Alaska.

INDIVIDUAL COURSES

The University of Alaska, Fairbanks, offers individual for-credit courses in: accounting (undergraduate); allied health (undergraduate); aviation technology (undergraduate); business/management (undergraduate); computer science (undergraduate); engineering (graduate); human services (undergraduate); liberal arts/general studies (undergraduate); mining technology (undergraduate); resource management (undergraduate); social work (undergraduate); teacher education (undergraduate and graduate).

UNIVERSITY OF ARIZONA

TUCSON, AZ 85719

The University of Arizona first offered a degree program via distance education in 1972.

Total enrollment in distance education programs (1992–93): 1,650.

The University of Arizona's College of Engineering and Mines pioneered video-based technical course offerings over 20 years ago. Today, VideoCampus offers engineering, optical science, education, foreign language, library science, and general studies course work via ITFS, the NTU (National Technological University) satellite network, cable television, and videotape. Beginning in spring 1994, pharmacy courses will be available on videotape.

DEGREE PROGRAMS

RELIABILITY AND QUALITY ENGINEERING

Professional Certificate in Reliability and Quality Engineering. Consists of 15 units of graduate level courses from the aerospace, mechanical engineering, systems, and industrial engineering departments.

Requirements: B.S. in engineering, mathematics, or physics and one undergraduate-level course in probability and statistics.

Degree/Certificate Awarded: Postsecondary certificate.

Availability: Open to the public; national.

Primary Methods of Course Delivery and Response: Cable television; satellite television; videocassette.

For more information, contact: Marsha Ham, Program Development Specialist, Extended University/VideoCampus, The University of Arizona, 1955 E. 6th St., Tucson, AZ 85719; Telephone: 800-955-8632 x 235; Fax: 602-621-3269.

RELIABILITY AND QUALITY ENGINEERING

Master of Science in Engineering With a Major in Reliability and Quality Engineering. All 15 units earned in the Professional Certificate Program apply to the master's degree. An additional 15 to 18 units of courses must be taken on campus.

Requirements: B.S. in engineering, mathematics, or physics.

Degree/Certificate Awarded: Master's—M.S.E.

Availability: Open to the public; national.

Primary Methods of Course Delivery and Response: Cable television; satellite television; videocassette.

On-Campus Component: 15 to 18 units must be completed on campus.

For more information, contact: Marsha Ham, Program Development Specialist,

Extended University/VideoCampus, The University of Arizona, 1955 E. 6th St., Tucson, AZ 85719; Telephone: 800-955-8632 x 234; Fax: 602-621-3269.

ELECTRICAL ENGINEERING
Master of Science in Engineering With a Major in Electrical Engineering. An average of 12 courses that can be applied toward the degree are offered each semester.

Requirements: B.S. in engineering or related field.

Degree/Certificate Awarded: Master's—M.S.E.

Availability: Open to the public; national.

Primary Methods of Course Delivery and Response: Cable television; satellite television; videocassette.

On-Campus Component: One semester.

For more information, contact: Marsha Ham, Program Development Specialist, Extended University/VideoCampus, The University of Arizona, 1955 E. 6th St., Tucson, AZ 85719; Telephone: 800-955-8632 x 234; Fax: 602-621-3269.

OPTICAL SCIENCES
Master of Science in Engineering With a Major in Optical Sciences. Two to three courses applying to the degree are offered each semester. As many as 15 units of course work can be completed via VideoCampus or NTU. Six or seven units can transfer from other institutions.

Requirements: B.S. in engineering, physics, mathematics, or related field.

Degree/Certificate Awarded: Master's—M.S.E.

Availability: Open to the public; national.

Primary Methods of Course Delivery and Response: Cable television; satellite television; videocassette.

On-Campus Component: One semester.

For more information, contact: Marsha Ham, Program Development Specialist, Extended University/VideoCampus, The University of Arizona, 1955 E. 6th St., Tucson, AZ 85719; Telephone: 800-955-8632 x 234; Fax: 602-621-3269.

PHARMACY
"ADVANCE" Doctor of Pharmacy. The four-year program includes 26 units of didactic course work and 25 units of clerkships. Students attend monthly meetings where they consult with the Pharm.D. coordinator and discuss course work with fellow students.

Requirements: B.S. in pharmacy; 2.5 GPA.

Degree/Certificate Awarded: Master's—Pharm.D.

Availability: Open to resident, registered Arizona pharmacists; statewide.

Primary Method of Course Delivery and Response: Videocassette.

For more information, contact: Marsha Ham, Program Development Specialist,

Extended University/VideoCampus, The University of Arizona, 1955 E. 6th St., Tucson, AZ 85719; Telephone: 800-955-8632 x 234; Fax: 602-621-3269.

LIBRARY SCIENCE: University of Arizona Cooperative Program in Library Science. Each academic semester, a minimum of two courses are offered via satellite or cable. Graduate credit may be earned only at approved sites.

Requirements: Same as for on-campus School of Library Science students.

Degree/Certificate Awarded: Master's—M.A.

Consortium Affiliation: WICHE Western Cooperative for Educational Telecommunication and Mind Extension University.

Availability: Open to the public; national—undergraduate correspondence throughout the U.S.; graduate at approved sites (primarily in the west).

Primary Methods of Course Delivery and Response: Commercial television; satellite television; videocassette.

On-Campus Component: Minimum of 12 semester hours.

Accreditation: American Library Association.

For more information, contact: Merrilyn S. Ridgeway, Program Development Specialist, Extended University, The University of Arizona, 1955 E. 6th St., Tucson, AZ 85719. Telephone: 800-955-UofA. Fax: 602-621-3279; Internet: MERRI@CCIT.ARIZONA.EDU; Bitnet: MERRI@CCIT.ARIZONA.EDU.

INDIVIDUAL COURSES

The University of Arizona offers individual for-credit courses in: engineering (undergraduate and graduate); foreign languages—beginning, intermediate (undergraduate); liberal arts/general studies (undergraduate); library science (undergraduate and graduate); pharmacy (undergraduate and graduate); teacher education (graduate).

UNIVERSITY OF CALGARY
CALGARY, ALBERTA T2N 1N4, CANADA

The University of Calgary first offered a degree program via distance education in 1989.
Total enrollment in distance education programs (1992–93): 400.

DEGREE PROGRAMS

SPECIAL EDUCATION
Professional Diploma in Special Education/ Gifted Education.

Requirements: B.E.D. degree; 2.5 GPA in last ten courses.

Degree/Certificate Awarded: Postsecondary certificate.

Availability: Open to the public; provincewide.

Primary Methods of Course Delivery and Response: Teleconferencing; telephone; videocassette.

On-Campus Component: One summer session (six weeks).

For more information, contact: Irene Meek, Manager, Distance Education, University of Calgary, Calgary, Alberta T2N 1N4, Canada; Telephone: 403-220-7346; Fax: 403-284-4879.

NURSING
Bachelor of Nursing Post Diploma Distance Education Programme.

Requirements: RN diploma; CPR certificate.

Degree/Certificate Awarded: Bachelor's—B.S.C.

Availability: Open to RNs; regional.

Primary Methods of Course Delivery and Response: Teleconferencing; telephone; videocassette.

For more information, contact: Irene Meek, Manager, Distance Education, University of Calgary, Calgary, Alberta T2N 1N4, Canada; Telephone: 403-220-7346; Fax: 403-284-4879.

INDIVIDUAL COURSES

The University of Calgary offers individual for-credit courses in: allied health (undergraduate); engineering (graduate); liberal arts/general studies (undergraduate); nursing (undergraduate); teacher education (undergraduate and graduate).

UNIVERSITY OF CALIFORNIA, SANTA BARBARA
SANTA BARBARA, CA 93106

The University of California, Santa Barbara, first offered a degree program via distance education in 1973.
Total enrollment in distance education programs (1992–93): 112.

Number graduating from distance programs (spring 1992): 28.

The distance education program at the University of California, Santa Barbara, is organized around a full-service remote facility. The Ventura Center offers student advisers, a computer lab for class writing assignments, a computer science laboratory, and a library research terminal.

DEGREE PROGRAMS

ELECTRICAL AND COMPUTER ENGINEERING
Off Campus Studies. Master's degree program.

Requirements: GRE; GPA.

Degree/Certificate Awarded: Master's—M.S.E.E.

Availability: Open to the public; regional.

Primary Methods of Course Delivery and Response: Electronic bulletin board; electronic mail; fax; ITFS; videocassette.

On-Campus Component: All final exams must be taken on campus.

For more information, contact: Judy Cotton, Student Affairs Officer, Off Campus Studies, University of California, Santa Barbara, CA 93106; Telephone: 805-893-4056; 805-893-4943.

COMPUTER SCIENCE
Off Campus Studies. Master's degree program.

Requirements: GRE; GPA.

Degree/Certificate Awarded: Master's—M.S.

Availability: Open to the public; regional.

Primary Methods of Course Delivery and Response: Electronic bulletin board, electronic mail; fax; ITFS; videocassette.

On-Campus Component: All final examinations must be taken on campus.

For more information, contact: Judy Cotton, Student Affairs Officer, Off Campus Studies, University of California, Santa Barbara, CA 93106; Telephone: 805-893-4056; 805-893-4943.

LIBERAL ARTS
Off Campus Studies. Upper-division classes in anthropology, sociology, English, history, law and society, psychology, political science, and interdisciplinary studies.

Requirements: Same as for on-campus students.

Degree/Certificate Awarded: Bachelor's—B.A.

Availability: Open to the public; regional.

Primary Methods of Course Delivery and Response: Fax; ITFS; telephone; videocassette.

For more information, contact: Susan Fauroat, Student Affairs Officer, Off Campus Studies/Ventura Center, 3585 Maple St. #112, Ventura, CA 93003; Telephone: 805-644-7261; Fax: 805-644-7268.

INDIVIDUAL COURSES

The University of California, Santa Barbara, offers an individual for-credit course in: engineering (graduate).

UNIVERSITY OF COLORADO AT BOULDER
BOULDER, CO 80309

The University of Colorado at Boulder first offered a degree program via distance education in 1983.
Total enrollment in distance education programs (1992–93): 790.

Number graduating from distance programs (spring 1992): 20.

The University of Colorado at Boulder's CATECS program offers graduate courses from the College of Engineering and Applied Science delivered directly to the workplace during the semester via live TV broadcast with interactive audio or videotape. Courses can be applied toward a master's degree or taken on a credit or noncredit basis for professional development. Courses taught in previous semesters are available for noncredit review through the tape library. Areas of study include engineering, computer science, telecommunications, and engineering management.

DEGREE PROGRAMS

AEROSPACE ENGINEERING
Master of Engineering in Aerospace Engineering. Includes fluid dynamics, astrodynamics and remote sensing, space structures, dynamics, systems and controls, and bioengineering.

Requirements: Bachelor's degree in engineering (or certain sciences) from an accredited institution; 3.0 GPA—applicants with a lower GPA may be required to take the GRE.

Degree/Certificate Awarded: Master's—M.E.

Availability: Open to the public; national.

Primary Methods of Course Delivery and Response: Electronic mail; fax; microwave television with interactive audio; satellite television; telephone; videocassette.

On-Campus Component: Oral defense of final project/thesis.

Accreditation: Accreditation Board for Engineering and Technology.

For more information, contact: Rae Boggs, Graduate Secretary, Department of Aerospace Engineering, University of Colorado–C.B. 429, Boulder, CO 80309-0429; Telephone: 303-492-6416; Fax: 303-492-2825.

AEROSPACE ENGINEERING
Master of Science in Aerospace Engineering. Includes fluid dynamics, astrodynamics and remote sensing, space structures, dynamics, systems and controls, and bioengineering.

Requirements: Same as for the M.E. except the GRE (general) and a 3.25 GPA are required.

Degree/Certificate Awarded: Master's—M.S.

Availability: Open to the public; national.

Primary Methods of Course Delivery and Response: Electronic mail; fax; microwave television with interactive audio; satellite television; telephone; videocassette.

On-Campus Component: Oral defense of final project/thesis.

Accreditation: Accreditation Board for Engineering and Technology.

For more information, contact: Rae Boggs, Graduate Secretary, Department of Aerospace Engineering, University of Colorado–C.B. 429, Boulder, CO 80309-0429; Telephone: 303-492-6416; Fax: 303-492-2825.

CIVIL AND ENVIRONMENTAL ENGINEERING

Master of Science in Civil and Environmental Engineering. Includes environmental and water resources, geoenvironmental engineering, structures and structural engineering, geotechnical engineering, construction engineering and management, and building systems engineering.

Requirements: 3.0 GPA—applicants with a GPA below 3.0 must take the GRE to be considered for provisional admission.

Degree/Certificate Awarded: Master's—M.S.

Availability: Open to the public; national.

Primary Methods of Course Delivery and Response: Electronic mail; fax; microwave television with interactive audio; satellite television; telephone; videocassette.

On-Campus Component: Oral defense of final project/thesis.

Accreditation: Accreditation Board for Engineering and Technology.

For more information, contact: Jan De May, Graduate Secretary, Department of Civil, Environmental, and Architectural Engineering, University of Colorado–C.B. 428, Boulder, CO 80309-0428; Telephone: 303-492-7316; Fax: 303-492-7317.

COMPUTER SCIENCE

Master of Engineering in Computer Science. Includes parallel processing, artificial intelligence, operating systems, theory of computation, programming languages, numerical computation, database systems, and software engineering.

Requirements: Bachelor's degree or equivalent from a comparable institution; 3.0 GPA—applicants with a GPA below 3.0 and above 2.75 or those lacking some admission requirements may be accepted as provisional degree students.

Degree/Certificate Awarded: Master's—M.E.

Availability: Open to the public; national.

Primary Methods of Course Delivery and Response: Electronic mail; fax; microwave television with interactive audio; satellite television; telephone; videocassette.

On-Campus Component: Oral defense of final project/thesis.

Accreditation: Accreditation Board for Engineering and Technology.

For more information, contact: Dotty Foerst, Graduate Secretary, Computer Science Department, University of Colorado–C.B. 430, Boulder, CO 80309-0430; Telephone: 303-492-6361; Fax: 303-492-2844.

COMPUTER SCIENCE

Master of Science in Computer Science. Includes parallel processing, artificial intelligence, operating systems, theory of computation, programming languages, numerical computation, database systems, and software engineering.

Requirements: Bachelor's degree or equivalent from a comparable institution; 3.0 GPA—applicants with a GPA below 3.0 and above 2.75 or those lacking some admission requirements may be accepted as provisional degree students.

Degree/Certificate Awarded: Master's—M.S.

Availability: Open to the public; national.

Primary Methods of Course Delivery and Response: Electronic mail; fax; microwave television with interactive audio; satellite television; telephone; videocassette.

On-Campus Component: Oral defense of final project/thesis.

Accreditation: Accreditation Board for Engineering and Technology.

For more information, contact: Dotty Foerst, Graduate Secretary, Computer Science Department, University of Colorado–C.B. 430, Boulder, CO 80309-0430; Telephone: 303-492-6361; Fax: 303-492-2844.

ELECTRICAL AND COMPUTER ENGINEERING

Master of Engineering in Electrical and Computer Engineering. Includes biomedical engineering, materials and quantum electronics, information systems, energy conversion and systems, robotics and control theory, optics and optoelectronics, fields and propagation, VLSI/design automation, digital signal processing, computers, and remote sensing.

Requirements: 3.0 GPA normally required from an accredited engineering program (science graduates with a good academic record and strong background in mathematics or science may be eligible); GRE may be required for applicants with GPA below 3.0.

Degree/Certificate Awarded: Master's—M.E.

Availability: Open to the public; national.

Primary Methods of Course Delivery and Response: Electronic mail; fax; microwave television with interactive audio; satellite television; telephone; videocassette.

On-Campus Component: Oral defense of final project/thesis.

Accreditation: Accreditation Board for Engineering and Technology.

For more information on the above programs, contact: Pam Wheeler, Graduate Secretary, Department of Electrical and Computer Engineering, University of Colorado–C.B. 425, Boulder, CO 80309-0425; Telephone: 303-492-7671; Fax: 303-492-2758.

ELECTRICAL AND COMPUTER ENGINEERING

Master of Science in Electrical and Computer Engineering. Includes biomedical engineering, materials and quantum electronics, information systems, energy conversion and systems, robotics and control theory, optics and optoelectronics, fields and propagation, VLSI/design automation, digital signal processing, computers, and remote sensing.

Requirements: Same as for M.E. applicants, except general GRE scores also required.

Degree/Certificate Awarded: Master's—M.S.

Availability: Open to the public; national.

Primary Methods of Course Delivery and Response: Electronic mail; fax; microwave television with interactive audio; satellite television; telephone; videocassette.

On-Campus Component: Oral defense of final project/thesis.

Accreditation: Accreditation Board for Engineering and Technology.

For more information on the above programs, contact: Pam Wheeler, Graduate Secretary, Department of Electrical and Computer Engineering, University of Colorado–C.B. 425, Boulder, CO 80309-0425; Telephone: 303-492-7671; Fax: 303-492-2758.

ENGINEERING MANAGEMENT
Master of Engineering in Engineering Management. Designed to provide both an intellectual foundation for the practice of technical management and practical information that can be immediately applied to the job.

Requirements: Bachelor's degree from an accredited engineering program (science and math graduates with excellent grades and strong backgrounds in both science and mathematics will be considered—degrees in engineering technology do not qualify); 3.0 GPA; GRE for provisional admission for applicants with a GPA below 3.0; two years professional work experience.

Degree/Certificate Awarded: Master's—M.E.

Availability: Open to the public; national.

Primary Methods of Course Delivery and Response: Electronic mail; fax; microwave television with interactive audio; satellite television; telephone; videocassette.

On-Campus Component: Oral defense of final project/thesis.

Accreditation: Accreditation Board for Engineering and Technology.

For more information, contact: Dee Zafiratos, Administrator, Engineering Management Program, University of Colorado–C.B. 435, Boulder, CO 80309-0435; Telephone: 303-492-2570.

MECHANICAL ENGINEERING
Master of Engineering in Mechanical Engineering. Includes engineering mathematics, fluid and thermal science, mechanics, design, manufacturing, and materials science.

Requirements: Bachelor's degree in engineering (or certain sciences) from an accredited institution; 3.0 GPA; GRE.

Degree/Certificate Awarded: Master's—M.E.

Availability: Open to the public; national.

Primary Methods of Course Delivery and Response: Electronic mail; fax; microwave television with interactive audio; satellite television; telephone; videocassette.

On-Campus Component: Oral defense of final project/thesis.

Accreditation: Accreditation Board for Engineering and Technology.

For more information, contact: Sharon Dominguez, Graduate Secretary, Department of Mechanical Engineering, University of Colorado–C.B. 427, Boulder, CO 80309-0427; Telephone: 303-492-7444; Fax: 303-492-3498.

MECHANICAL ENGINEERING
Master of Science in Mechanical Engineering. Includes engineering mathematics, fluid and thermal science, mechanics, design, manufacturing, and materials science.

Requirements: Bachelor's degree in engineering (or certain sciences) from an accredited institution; 3.0 GPA; GRE.

Degree/Certificate Awarded: Master's—M.S.

Availability: Open to the public; national.

Primary Methods of Course Delivery and Response: Electronic mail; fax; microwave television with interactive audio; satellite television; telephone; videocassette.

On-Campus Component: Oral defense of final project/thesis.

Accreditation: Accreditation Board for Engineering and Technology.

For more information, contact: Sharon Dominguez, Graduate Secretary, Department of Mechanical Engineering, University of Colorado–C.B. 427, Boulder, CO 80309-0427; Telephone: 303-492-7444; Fax: 303-492-3498.

TELECOMMUNICATIONS
Master of Engineering in Telecommunications. Includes data and computer networks, mobile and secure communications, fiber optics, ISDN, telecommunication and telephone systems, traffic and queuing theory, telecommunications business (management, planning, information systems), and telecommunications policy (regulatory, economic, and legal aspects).

Requirements: Bachelor's degree from an accredited engineering program; science graduates with a good academic record and strong background in mathematics, science, or telecommunications may be eligible; GRE or GMAT for applicants with GPA below 3.0.

Degree/Certificate Awarded: Master's—M.E.

Availability: Open to the public; national.

Primary Methods of Course Delivery and Response: Electronic mail; fax; microwave television with interactive audio; satellite television; telephone; videocassette.

On-Campus Component: Oral defense of final project/thesis.

Accreditation: Accreditation Board for Engineering and Technology.

For more information, contact: Esther Sparn, Interdisciplinary Telecommunications Program, University of Colorado–C.B. 530, Boulder, CO 80309-0530; Telephone: 303-492-8916; Fax: 303-492-8233.

TELECOMMUNICATIONS
Master of Science in Telecommunications. Includes data and computer networks, mobile and secure communications, fiber optics, ISDN, telecommunication and telephone systems, traffic and queuing theory, telecommunications business

(management, planning, information systems), and telecommunications policy (regulatory, economic, and legal aspects).

Requirements: Relevant undergraduate experience, training background in telecommunications, or genuine interest in or aptitude for the field; GRE or GMAT for applicants with GPA below 3.0.

Degree/Certificate Awarded: Master's—M.S.

Availability: Open to the public; national.

Primary Methods of Course Delivery and Response: Electronic mail; fax; microwave television with interactive audio; satellite television; telephone; videocassette.

On-Campus Component: Oral defense of final project/thesis.

Accreditation: Accreditation Board for Engineering and Technology.

For more information, contact: Esther Sparn, Interdisciplinary Telecommunications Program, University of Colorado–C.B. 530, Boulder, CO 80309-0530; Telephone: 303-492-8916; Fax: 303-492-8233.

SOFTWARE ENGINEERING
Master of Engineering in Software Engineering. Intended to provide a source of high-quality software developers through a partnership between academia and industry.

Requirements: B.S. in computer engineering or computer science; at least one semester in software systems development involving both theory and project experience or one year experience as a software engineer in industry or B.A./B.S. in another field and two years experience as a software engineer in industry.

Degree/Certificate Awarded: Master's—M.E.

Availability: Open to the public; national.

Primary Methods of Course Delivery and Response: Electronic mail; fax; microwave television with interactive audio; satellite television; telephone; videocassette.

On-Campus Component: Project (12 credit hours)—usually one to two semesters of weekly attendance.

Accreditation: Accreditation Board for Engineering and Technology.

For more information, contact: Professor William M. Waite, Chairman, Department of Electrical and Computer Engineering, University of Colorado–C.B. 425, Boulder, CO 80309-0425; Telephone: 303-492-3511; Internet: waite@boulder.colorado.edu.

INDIVIDUAL COURSES

The University of Colorado at Boulder offers individual for-credit courses in: business/management (graduate); computer science (graduate); engineering (graduate); environmental health and safety (graduate); telecommunications (graduate).

UNIVERSITY OF COLORADO AT COLORADO SPRINGS
COLORADO SPRINGS, CO 80933-7150

The University of Colorado at Colorado Springs first offered a degree program via distance education in 1992.
Total enrollment in distance education programs (1992–93): 250.

The instructional television network at the University of Colorado at Colorado Springs, CU-Net, consists of ITFS, fiber optics, satellite, and cable technologies. Telecourses are offered via ITFS and cable to residents of the Pikes Peak region. Resident instruction and distance education classes are offered over the systemwide CU Fiber-Net fiber optics interconnect, and teleconferences are received and distributed using satellite technology. Telecourses are offered by every college of the university, at both lower-division and upper-division undergraduate and graduate levels, and courses required in the coordinated graduate degree programs are a priority on the fiber system. CU-Net has also produced an eight-hour Certificate in Early Reading Instruction, which airs nationally over Mind Extension University.

DEGREE PROGRAM

READING
Certificate in Early Reading Instruction. Eight-hour certificate designed to instruct parents and teachers of young children in the strategies, methods, and materials needed to create literate environments for children.

Requirements: Bachelor's degree.

Degree/Certificate Awarded: Postsecondary certificate.

Availability: Open to the public; national.

Primary Methods of Course Delivery and Response: Local cable television; satellite television.

For more information, contact: Linda Aaker, Program Coordinator, CU-Net, University of Colorado at Colorado Springs, P.O. Box 7150, Colorado Springs, CO 80933-7150; Telephone: 719-593-3597; Fax: 719-593-3362; Internet: LKAAKER@UCCS.EDU; Bitnet: LKAAKER@BitNet.

INDIVIDUAL COURSES

The University of Colorado at Colorado Springs offers individual for-credit courses in: accounting (undergraduate and graduate); business/management (undergraduate); engineering (undergraduate and graduate); environmental health and safety (undergraduate); foreign languages (undergraduate); liberal arts/general studies (undergraduate); space studies (undergraduate and graduate); teacher education (undergraduate and graduate).

UNIVERSITY OF DELAWARE
NEWARK, DE 19716

The University of Delaware first offered a degree program via distance education in 1988.

Total enrollment in distance education programs (1992–93): 872.

Number graduating from distance programs (spring 1992): 2.

The University of Delaware's FOCUS/Distance Learning system serves adult students whose work schedules, geographic location, or personal responsibilities limit their access to on-campus classes. A number of academic departments participate at both the undergraduate and graduate levels, offering everything from English to engineering and from chemistry to child development. Every semester, selected on-campus courses are taught and videotaped in the university's ITV classrooms. At the end of each week, lecture videotapes and class handouts are sent to site coordinators for distribution at work sites where participants are enrolled. Exams are proctored at the work site or a convenient university location. Students without participating work sites can enroll as individuals by paying a video handling fee. The university also offers engineering courses through National Technological University's satellite system.

DEGREE PROGRAM

NURSING
Bachelor of Science in Nursing for Registered Nurses. Designed for registered nurses working toward the B.S.N. degree. Contains all the required nursing lecture courses and many required support courses on videotape.

Requirements: Must be a licensed registered nurse; must meet requirements for transfer students.

Degree/Certificate Awarded: Bachelor's—B.S.N.

Availability: Open to registered nurses; regional.

Primary Methods of Course Delivery and Response: Videocassette.

On-Campus Component: Currently one weekend, will change to three weekends in near future.

Accreditation: National League for Nursing.

For more information, contact: Madeline Lambrecht, Assistant Chairperson, College of Nursing, University of Delaware, McDowell Hall, Newark, DE 19716; Telephone: 302-831-8368; Fax: 302-831-2382.

INDIVIDUAL COURSES

The University of Delaware offers individual for-credit courses in: business/management (undergraduate); engineering (undergraduate and graduate); liberal arts/general studies (undergraduate); nursing (undergraduate); teacher education (undergraduate).

UNIVERSITY OF HOUSTON
HOUSTON, TX 77204

The University of Houston first offered a degree program via distance education in 1984.
Total enrollment in distance education programs (1992–93): 816.

The University of Houston's Instructional Television (ITV) classes are fully accredited graduate and undergraduate courses taught live and interactively via closed-circuit television. Students at receive sites view classes on monitors and interact with the instructor and other receive site students by microphones or telephone. Since 1984, more than 2,700 students in 138 graduate and undergraduate courses have enrolled in ITV courses at receive sites throughout the Houston area. ITV is available at the North Houston Institute, the Texas Medical Center Institute, the West Houston Institute at Cinco Ranch, and the Brazosport Independent School District Media Center as well as a number of school and corporate sites in the Houston area.

DEGREE PROGRAMS

ELECTRICAL ENGINEERING
Master's Degree in Electrical Engineering with Computer Specialization.

Requirements: Same as for on-campus College of Engineering students.

Degree/Certificate Awarded: Master's—M.A.

Availability: Open to the public; local.

Primary Methods of Course Delivery and Response: Closed-circuit television; two-way audio and one-way TV transmission.

For more information, contact: Sandy Frieden, Director of Programming, Continuing Education and Off Campus Institutes, University of Houston, Houston, TX 77204-2162; Telephone: 713-395-2800; Fax: 713-395-2629.

INDUSTRIAL ENGINEERING
Master's Degree in Industrial Engineering with an Engineering Management Specialization.

Requirements: Same as for on-campus College of Engineering students.

Degree/Certificate Awarded: Master's—M.A.

Availability: Open to the public; local.

Primary Methods of Course Delivery and Response: Closed-circuit television; two-way audio and one-way TV transmission.

For more information, contact: Sandy Frieden, Director of Programming, Continuing Education and Off Campus Institutes, University of Houston, Houston, TX 77204-2162; Telephone: 713-395-2800; Fax: 713-395-2629.

INDIVIDUAL COURSES

The University of Houston offers individual for-credit courses in: engineering (graduate); liberal arts/general studies (graduate); teacher education (graduate).

UNIVERSITY OF IDAHO
MOSCOW, ID 83843

The University of Idaho first offered a degree program via distance education in 1975.
Total enrollment in distance education programs (1992–93): 975.

Number graduating from distance programs (spring 1992): 33.

The University of Idaho's video outreach program offers master's degree courses in various engineering disciplines via videotape, satellite, and microwave. All courses carry resident credit and meet all degree requirements.

DEGREE PROGRAM

ENGINEERING
Video Outreach Program. Master's-level program in engineering and continuing professional development via videotape.

Requirements: Same as for on-campus students.

Degree/Certificate Awarded: Master's—M.S.

Availability: Open to the public; national.

Primary Methods of Course Delivery and Response: Electronic mail; fax; microwave; satellite television; telephone; videocassette.

Accreditation: Northwest Association of Schools and Colleges; Accreditation Board for Engineering and Technology.

For more information, contact: Dr. A. L. Rigas, Director, Engineering Outreach, University of Idaho, 40 Janssen Engineering Bldg., Moscow, ID 83843; Telephone: 208-885-6373; Fax: 208-885-6165; Internet: Outreach @ newton.eugrad.uidaho.edu.

INDIVIDUAL COURSES

The University of Idaho offers individual for-credit courses in: computer science (graduate); engineering (graduate).

UNIVERSITY OF ILLINOIS AT URBANA-CHAMPAIGN
CHAMPAIGN, IL 61820

The University of Illinois at Urbana-Champaign first offered a degree program via distance education in 1973.

Total enrollment in distance education programs (1992–93): 300.

Number graduating from distance programs (spring 1992): 18.

The University of Illinois at Urbana-Champaign offers distance education courses in engineering at the graduate and advanced undergraduate levels, both as part of master's degree programs and for professional development. Campus courses are videotaped for viewing at off-campus locations. At least three enrollments at each site are required. Homework assignments, proctored examinations, and interactive sessions are required. Admission to the master's degree programs is competitive. Only a limited number of courses taken prior to admission can be petitioned into a degree program. Individuals wishing to pursue a master's degree program should inquire and apply for admission as early as possible.

DEGREE PROGRAMS

MECHANICS
Master of Science in Theoretical and Applied Mechanics (TAM). Nine units (36 semester hours) of credit with at least five in TAM and five at the 400 level.

Requirements: Evidence of adequate preparation; B average.

Degree/Certificate Awarded: Master's—M.S.

Availability: Open to the public; regional.

Primary Methods of Course Delivery and Response: Telephone; videocassette.

For more information, contact: Dr. Linda Krute, Coordinator, Engineering Programs, Continuing Engineering Education, University of Illinois at Urbana-Champaign, 422 Engineering Hall, 1308 W. Green St., Urbana, IL 61801: Telephone: 217-333-6634; Fax: 217-333-0015.

MECHANICAL ENGINEERING
Master of Science in Mechanical Engineering. Eight units (32 semester hours) of credit with a thesis or nine units without a thesis.

Requirements: Adequate preparation; B average.

Degree/Certificate Awarded: Master's—M.S.

Availability: Open to the public; statewide.

Primary Methods of Course Delivery and Response: Telephone; videocassette.

For more information, contact: Dr. Linda Krute, Coordinator, Engineering Programs, Continuing Engineering Education, University of Illinois at Urbana-Champaign, 422 Engineering Hall, 1308 W. Green St., Urbana, IL 61801: Telephone: 217-333-6634; Fax: 217-333-0015.

ENGINEERING
Master of Science in General Engineering. Eight units (32 semester hours) of credit with a thesis or nine units without a thesis and with a project design.

Requirements: Evidence of adequate preparation; B average.

Degree/Certificate Awarded: Master's—M.S.

Availability: Open to the public; statewide.

Primary Methods of Course Delivery and Response: Telephone; videocassette.

For more information, contact: Dr. Linda Krute, Coordinator, Engineering Programs, Continuing Engineering Education, University of Illinois at Urbana-Champaign, 422 Engineering Hall, 1308 W. Green St., Urbana, IL 61801: Telephone: 217-333-6634; Fax: 217-333-0015.

ELECTRICAL ENGINEERING
Master of Science in Electrical Engineering. Eight units (32 semester hours) of credit required, including a required thesis and five units at the 400 level.

Requirements: B average; GRE.

Degree/Certificate Awarded: Master's—M.S.

Availability: Open to the public; statewide.

Primary Methods of Course Delivery and Response: Telephone; videocassette.

For more information, contact: Dr. Linda Krute, Coordinator, Engineering Programs, Continuing Engineering Education, University of Illinois at Urbana-Champaign, 422 Engineering Hall, 1308 W. Green St., Urbana, IL 61801: Telephone: 217-333-6634; Fax: 217-333-0015.

NUCLEAR ENGINEERING
Master of Science in Nuclear Engineering. Eight units (32 semester hours) of credit required, including a thesis.

Requirements: Evidence of adequate preparation; B average.

Degree/Certificate Awarded: Master's—M.S.

Availability: Open to the public; national.

Primary Methods of Course Delivery and Response: Telephone; videocassette.

For more information, contact: Dr. Linda Krute, Coordinator, Engineering Programs, Continuing Engineering Education, University of Illinois at Urbana-Champaign, 422 Engineering Hall, 1308 W. Green St., Urbana, IL 61801: Telephone: 217-333-6634; Fax: 217-333-0015.

INDIVIDUAL COURSES

The University of Illinois at Urbana-Champaign offers individual for-credit courses in: engineering (graduate).

UNIVERSITY OF IOWA
IOWA CITY, IA 52242

The University of Iowa first offered a degree program via distance education in 1986.
Total enrollment in distance education programs (1992–93): 807.

The University of Iowa has offered distance learning since the early years of this century. The range of service is either relatively local (within 35 miles) or to multiple sites statewide.

DEGREE PROGRAMS

COMPUTER SCIENCE
Master of Science in Computer Science.

Requirements: Generally, a background equivalent to a B.A. or B.S. in computer science; other requirements same as for on-campus graduate students.

Degree/Certificate Awarded: Master's—M.S.

Availability: Open to corporate subscribers; open to the public on a space-available basis; local.

Primary Method of Course Delivery and Response: Closed-circuit television.

On-Campus Component: One graduate-level seminar.

For more information, contact: Wayne Prophet, Assistant Director/Off-Campus Courses and Programs, Credit Programs, University of Iowa, Iowa City, IA 52242; Telephone: 319-335-2050; Fax: 319-335-2740; Internet: Wayne-Prophet@Uiowa.edu.

LIBERAL STUDIES
Bachelor of Liberal Studies.

Requirements: Must have completed 62 undergraduate credits.

Degree/Certificate Awarded: Bachelor's—B.L.S.

Availability: Open to the public; national.

Primary Methods of Course Delivery and Response: Public television; teleconferencing; videocassette.

Accreditation: North Central Association of Colleges and Schools.

For more information, contact: Scot Wilcox, Educational Adviser, Department of Continuing Education, University of Iowa, 116 International Ctr., Iowa City, IA 52242; Telephone: 319-335-2575.

INDIVIDUAL COURSES

The University of Iowa offers individual for-credit courses in: computer science (undergraduate and graduate); liberal arts/general studies (undergraduate and graduate); nursing (undergraduate and graduate); social work (undergraduate and graduate); teacher education (undergraduate and graduate).

ARTHETTA TAYLOR

Age: 46

Institution: University of Kentucky

Courses taken: Five classes in educational administration: educational leadership, foundations of inquiry, cohort induction, quantitative inquiry, theories of communication.

Academic goals and achievements: Taylor has already earned three degrees from Marshall University, including an A.B. in vocational home economics and an M.A. in foods and nutrition, plus an M.A. in educational administration. Currently she is earning her Ed.D. in educational administration through the University of Kentucky's distance learning program.

"I live just across the West Virginia/Kentucky border and commute about 40 minutes to UK's Ashland site in Kentucky for my classes. When I first heard about the University of Kentucky's distance learning program, I saw it not just as an opportunity to fulfill my lifelong dream of earning my doctorate, but also as a way to experience firsthand the kind of technology that our rural county needs to improve educational opportunities.

"I am general supervisor for the Wayne County Board of Education, where, among other things, I'm responsible for staff development and computer coordination. The median per capita income in our county is $9400. I believe if more of our citizens could take advantage of the opportunities that distance learning technology offers, they could get off welfare and improve their skills and income earning ability. Once we improve the skills of our work force, I think more businesses would be attracted to the area and it would improve our economy.

"I am very excited about the new possibilities distance learning allows. The equipment is so easy that a second grader—literally—could operate it. I am in a classroom with five people, but I notice that at other sites in Owensboro and Lexington there are more. The technology is compressed video via telephone lines, and the quality is excellent—virtually indistinguishable from regular television signals. If you have to ask a question, the camera reacts instantaneously; it flashes around the room and seems to be sensitive to noise because it automatically zeroes in on the person who is speaking (or sometimes just rustling papers). It's almost like being in the classroom. If you have to give a presentation, there's a palette at the podium that you manipulate with a stylus. It has little icons on it that make it a snap to operate.

"In my computer class we can turn in our papers either via electronic mail (it can read an ASCII file) or, if we want to add stylistic formatting, via fax.

"When the cost of this technology comes down, I see all sorts of exciting benefits for public schools in rural communities. For example, we'd only have to get one teacher for the whole county who could teach Japanese. It would also be a way to let students in physics classes across the county interact. I've been in school since I was five years old, but I've never experienced anything as exciting as this—it can benefit all areas of education in both schools and business training."

UNIVERSITY OF KENTUCKY
LEXINGTON, KY 40506-0032

The University of Kentucky first offered a degree program via distance education in 1991.

Total enrollment in distance education programs (1992–93): 311.

The University of Kentucky utilizes compressed-video and satellite delivery systems to offer graduate and professional degree programs, select undergraduate and graduate courses, and continuing education opportunities to the Commonwealth of Kentucky and beyond. The University of Kentucky Community College system, public libraries, government agencies, and public schools all serve as extended-campus locations with individual coordinators based at each site. The university has four remote compressed-video sites across the state; six additional sites are planned. In addition, the university works closely with Kentucky Educational Television's STAR Channels network, with over 1,600 down-link sites, to deliver satellite programming throughout the state. Doctoral students at four Graduate Program Sites have remote, direct access to the University of Kentucky mainframe computer for E-Mail and for searching the library catalog and electronic databases. Extended-campus programs are coordinated by the graduate school through a network of site directors and on-campus support units.

DEGREE PROGRAMS

ENGINEERING
Master of Engineering. Thirty hours of course work in a general interest area.

Requirements: Same as for on-campus graduate students; bachelor's degree in engineering.

Degree/Certificate Awarded: Master's—M.E.

Availability: Open to the public; statewide.

Primary Methods of Course Delivery and Response: Compressed-video television.

For more information, contact: Dr. John A. Walker, Associate Dean, College of Engineering, University of Kentucky, 177 Anderson Hall, Lexington, KY 40506-0046; Telephone: 606-257-6262 ext. 205; Fax: 606-257-4922.

MINING ENGINEERING
Master's Degree in Mining Engineering. Directed primarily toward practicing engineers in mining or related fields.

Requirements: Same as for on-campus graduate students.

Degree/Certificate Awarded: Master's—M.Min.E.

Availability: Open to the public; national.

Primary Method of Course Delivery and Response: Satellite television.

Accreditation: Southern Association of Colleges and Schools.

For more information, contact: Constance Baird, Director, Extended Campus Programs, University of Kentucky, 1A Frazee Hall, Lexington, KY 40506-0031; Telephone: 606-257-3377; Fax: 606-257-5171.

FAMILY STUDIES
Master of Science in Family Studies—Family Economics and Management. Focuses on family economic well-being and management.

Requirements: 2.5 undergraduate GPA; 900 verbal and quantitative GREs.

Degree/Certificate Awarded: Master's—M.S.

Availability: Open to the public; statewide.

Primary Methods of Course Delivery and Response: Satellite television.

On-Campus Component: One semester.

For more information, contact: Dr. Raymond E. Forgue, Chair, Family Studies, University of Kentucky, Lexington, KY 40506; Telephone: 606-257-7756; Fax: 606-257-4095; Internet: FAM004@UKCC.UKY.EDU.

SPECIAL EDUCATION
Training Rural Educators in Kentucky Through Distance Learning. Graduate program (master's, specialist certification, or rank) for teachers of students with severe disabilities or teachers in early childhood special education.

Requirements: Bachelor's degree in education or related field.

Degree/Certificate Awarded: Postsecondary certificate, M.S., E.D.S.

Availability: Open to special educators or service delivery personnel; regional.

Primary Methods of Course Delivery and Response: Compressed-video television; satellite television; site visitation and supervision; telephone.

Accreditation: Southern Association of Colleges and Schools, Kentucky Department of Education, National Council for the Accreditation of Teacher Education.

For more information, contact: Belva C. Collins, Ed.D., Project Director and Assistant Professor, Department of Special Education, University of Kentucky, 229 Taylor Education Bldg., Lexington, KY 40506-0001; Telephone: 606-257-8591.

EDUCATION
Ed.D. in Educational Administration and Supervision/Educational Policy Studies and Evaluation. Theory and practice of transformational leadership/educational policy studies with an emphasis on higher education.

Requirements: Same as for on-campus doctoral students.

Degree/Certificate Awarded: Doctorate—Ed.D.

Availability: Open to school practitioners holding certification; three compressed-video sites in Kentucky.

Primary Method of Course Delivery and Response: Compressed-video television.

Accreditation: Southern Association of Colleges and Schools.

For more information, contact: Dr. Susan J. Scollay, Director of Graduate Studies, Administration and Supervision, University of Kentucky, 111B Dickey Hall, Lexington, KY 40506-0017; Telephone: 606-257-7834; Fax: 606-258-1046.

EDUCATION

Educational Policy Studies and Evaluation—Higher Education. Study of the various subsystems in higher education (e.g., administration, faculty, students, legal).

Requirements: 2.5 undergraduate GPA; GRE; faculty analysis.

Degree/Certificate Awarded: Doctorate—Ed.D.

Availability: Open to the public; statewide.

Primary Methods of Course Delivery and Response: Compressed-video television; computer conferencing; electronic mail; fax; telephone; videoconferencing.

On-Campus Component: One or two summer sessions.

For more information, contact: Dr. Clinton Collins, Director of Graduate Studies, Educational Policy Studies and Evaluation, University of Kentucky, 128 Taylor Education Bldg., Lexington, KY 40506-0001. Telephone: 606-247-4795. Fax: 606-258-1046.

INDIVIDUAL COURSES

The University of Kentucky offers individual for-credit courses in: agriculture (graduate); allied health (undergraduate); engineering (graduate); family studies (graduate); library science (graduate); nursing (undergraduate and graduate); pharmacy (graduate); teacher education (graduate).

UNIVERSITY OF MARYLAND UNIVERSITY COLLEGE
COLLEGE PARK, MD 20742-1628

The University of Maryland University College first offered a degree program via distance education in 1972.

Total enrollment in distance education programs (1992–93): 13,377.

Number graduating from distance programs (spring 1992): 137.

The University of Maryland University College utilizes a variety of technologies and formats to provide maximum flexibility for distance students. Electronic media include instructional television, video enhancement using cable and VCR distribution, on-line conferencing, computer-guided instructional programming, audio teleconferencing and telephone networks, voice mail, fax, and audiocassettes. All courses also have a strong print-based component. Degree completion programs are available in behavioral and social sciences, business and management studies, computer and information systems, fire science, management, nuclear science, paralegal studies, and technology and management.

DEGREE PROGRAMS

BUSINESS

Instructional Television Degree Completion Program. Offers selected computer and business and management curricula through distributed classroom model.

Requirements: High school diploma from a regionally accredited or state-approved school or 225 GED with no score below 40; 2.0 cumulative GPA in all college-level work at other regionally accredited colleges or universities.

Degree/Certificate Awarded: Bachelor's—B.S., B.A.

Availability: Open to the public; statewide.

Primary Methods of Course Delivery and Response: Closed-circuit television; fax; telephone.

For more information, contact: Lolethia L. Lomax-Frazier, Director of Enrollment Services (Acting), Admission UMUC, University of Maryland University College, University Blvd. at Adelphi Rd., College Park, MD 20742; Telephone: 301-985-7265; Fax: 301-985-7364.

MANAGEMENT

UMUC degree with primary concentration in management, integrating contemporary theory and practice in the field. Includes diversity, leadership, problem solving, ethics, and global environment.

Requirements: High school diploma from a regionally accredited or state-approved school or 225 GED with no score below 40; 2.0 cumulative GPA in all college-level work at other regionally accredited colleges or universities.

Degree/Certificate Awarded: Bachelor's—B.A., B.S.

Consortium Affiliation: National Universities Degree Consortium.

Availability: Open to the public; national.

Primary Methods of Course Delivery and Response: Cable television; fax; satellite television; telephone; videocassette; voice mail conferencing.

For more information, contact: Rita Tschiffely, Coordinator, Independent Learning, Undergraduate Programs, University of Maryland University College, University Blvd. at Adelphi Rd., College Park, MD 20742; Telephone: 301-985-7722; Fax: 301-985-4615.

NUCLEAR SCIENCE
Nuclear Science Engineering Program. Degree courses delivered through multimedia instruction to personnel in the nuclear industry.

Requirements: High school diploma from a regionally accredited or state-approved school or 225 GED with no score below 40; 2.0 cumulative GPA in all college-level work at other regionally accredited colleges or universities.

Degree/Certificate Awarded: Bachelor's—B.S.

Consortium Affiliation: Consortium of University of Maryland University College and participating nuclear utilities. Headquarters: University of Maryland University College.

Availability: Open to nuclear industry personnel; national.

Primary Methods of Course Delivery and Response: Computer conferencing; electronic mail; fax; interactive PC lessons; on-line quiz system.

For more information, contact: Thomas Janke, Assistant Vice President, Special Programs, Nuclear Science Program, University of Maryland University College, University Blvd. at Adelphi Rd., College Park, MD 20742; Telephone: 301-985-7881; Fax: 301-985-7937.

OPEN LEARNING PROGRAM
Behavioral and social sciences, fire science, general science, humanities, and technology and management courses offered through various delivery formats.

Requirements: High school diploma from a regionally accredited or state-approved school or 225 GED with no score below 40; 2.0 cumulative GPA in all college-level work at other regionally accredited colleges or universities.

Degree/Certificate Awarded: Bachelor's—B.S. or B.A.

Consortium Affiliation: Some courses offered through the International University Consortium, or Open Learning Fire Service Program, National Fire Academy.

Availability: Open to the public; fire science offered regionally.

Primary Methods of Course Delivery and Response: Audiocassette; audio teleconferencing; cable television; computer conferencing; electronic bulletin board; electronic mail; fax; public television; telephone; videocassette.

On-Campus Component: For some courses, class attendance required at orientation and exams.

For more information, contact: Ruthann Fagan, Assistant Dean, Open Learning,

Undergraduate Programs, University of Maryland University College, University Blvd. at Adelphi Rd., College Park, MD 20742; Telephone: 301-985-7722; Fax: 301-985-4615; Bitnet: Fagan@UMUC.UMD.EDU.

PARALEGAL STUDIES
Law-related courses to prepare students for positions in law firms, government agencies, corporations, trade associations, banking, and real estate.

Requirements: High school diploma from a regionally accredited or state-approved school or 225 GED with no score below 40; 2.0 cumulative GPA in all college-level work at other regionally accredited colleges or universities.

Degree/Certificate Awarded: Bachelor's—B.A. or B.S. Also paralegal document for completion of ten courses.

Availability: Open to the public; national.

Primary Methods of Course Delivery and Response: Fax; telephone.

For more information, contact: Hannah Kaufman, Program Manager, Paralegal Studies, Undergraduate Programs, University of Maryland University College, University Blvd. at Adelphi Rd., College Park, MD 20742; Telephone: 301-985-7733; Fax: 301-985-4615; Bitnet: KAUFMAN@UMUC.UMD.EDU.

INDIVIDUAL COURSES

The University of Maryland University College offers individual for-credit courses in: accounting (undergraduate); behavior and social science (undergraduate); business/management (undergraduate); computer science (undergraduate); economics (undergraduate); English (undergraduate); fire science (undergraduate); general science (undergraduate); government (undergraduate); liberal arts/general studies (undergraduate); marketing (undergraduate); nuclear science (undergraduate); psychology (undergraduate); technology and management (undergraduate).

UNIVERSITY OF MASSACHUSETTS AT AMHERST
AMHERST, MA 01003

The University of Massachusetts at Amherst first offered a degree program via distance education in 1976.

Total enrollment in distance education programs (1992–93): 1,206.

Number graduating from distance programs (spring 1992): 22.

As part of the College of Engineering at the University of Massachusetts at Amherst, the Video Instruction Program videotapes and broadcasts courses taught by resident graduate faculty before an on-campus audience and delivers them weekly to off-campus students. Semester-length courses may be taken for credit or audit and as part of a graduate degree program in either electrical and computer engineering or engineering management. Shorter courses, used primarily for training purposes, are also available. In addition, the Video Instruction Program broadcasts courses over Ku-band satellite through affiliation with National Technological University (NTU).

DEGREE PROGRAM

ENGINEERING
Video Instructional Program (VIP). Videotape and satellite broadcast of graduate courses in engineering and related areas to off-campus students.

Requirements: Degree-enrolled students—same requirements as on-campus students; non-degree students need only submit registration form and payment.

Degree/Certificate Awarded: Master's—M.S.

Availability: Open to the public (but most students are from industry); national.

Primary Methods of Course Delivery and Response: Electronic mail; fax; satellite television; telephone; videocassette.

For more information, contact: Elisabeth D. Bowman, Marketing Coordinator, Video Instructional Program, University of Massachusetts at Amherst, 113 Marcus Hall, Amherst, MA 01003; Telephone: 413-545-0063; Fax: 413-545-1227; Internet: Bowman@ECS.UMASS.EDU.

INDIVIDUAL COURSES

The University of Massachusetts at Amherst offers individual for-credit courses in: business/management (graduate); computer science (graduate); engineering (undergraduate and graduate); environmental health and safety (graduate); nursing (graduate).

UNIVERSITY OF MISSOURI–ROLLA
ROLLA, MO 65401

The University of Missouri–Rolla first offered a degree program via distance education in 1985.
Total enrollment in distance education programs (1992–93): 220.

Number graduating from distance programs (spring 1992): 30.

The University of Missouri–Rolla offers engineering management courses and a graduate degree through National Technological University. The University of Missouri–Rolla also offers a graduate degree via fiber optic network to students in the Kansas City area.

DEGREE PROGRAMS

ENGINEERING MANAGEMENT
National Technological University Master of Science Degree Program in Engineering Management. A minimum of 12 engineering management credits out of 33 total credits required must be core and elective courses taken through the National Technological University.

Requirements: Prefer B.S. or other degree in engineering, chemistry, mathematics, physics, or computer science from an accredited institution (not necessarily Accreditation Board for Engineering and Technology in the case of engineering) or the equivalent from a foreign institution; 2.5 GPA; two years work experience in an engineering environment; computer literacy.

Degree/Certificate Awarded: Master's—M.S.

Consortium Affiliation: National Technological University (NTU).

Availability: Open to NTU corporate members and schools; national.

Primary Methods of Course Delivery and Response: Compressed-video television; satellite television.

Accreditation: Accreditation Board for Engineering and Technology, Commission on Institutions of Higher Education of the North Central Association of Colleges and Schools.

For more information, contact: Douglas M. Yeager, Vice President, Marketing, 700 Centre Ave., Fort Collins, CO 80526; Telephone: 303-484-6050; Fax: 303-484-0668.

ENGINEERING/COMPUTER SCIENCE
University of Missouri–Rolla Graduate Program at University of Missouri—Kansas City Video Network. At least 11 three-hour courses selected from engineering management, engineering, and computer science topics, or at least eight such courses and a thesis.

Requirements: 3.0 GPA; TOEFL; GRE.

Degree/Certificate Awarded: Master's—M.S.

Availability: Open to the public; Kansas City area.

Primary Method of Course Delivery and Response: Compressed-video television.

Accreditation: Accreditation Board for Engineering and Technology.

For more information, contact: Dr. Madison Daily, Acting Chairman and Kansas City Advisor, Engineering Management, University of Missouri–Rolla, 230 Engineering Management Dept., Rolla, MO 65401; Telephone: 314-341-4571; Fax: 314-341-6567.

INDIVIDUAL COURSES

The University of Missouri–Rolla offers individual for-credit courses in: computer science (graduate); engineering (graduate).

UNIVERSITY OF MONTANA
MISSOULA, MT 59812

The University of Montana first offered a degree program via distance education in 1988.

Total enrollment in distance education programs (1992–93): 51.

Number graduating from distance programs (spring 1992): 9.

The University of Montana offers courses primarily through compressed interactive video supplemented by audio conferencing and computer conferencing.

DEGREE PROGRAM

BUSINESS ADMINISTRATION
Billings M.B.A. Delivered partially electronically and partially face-to-face.

Requirements: Traditional master's level: GPA; GRE; letters of recommendation; work experience.

Degree/Certificate Awarded: Master's—M.B.A.

Availability: Open to individuals accessible to Billings, MT; local.

Primary Methods of Course Delivery and Response: Compressed-video television; computer conferencing; fax; telephone.

For more information, contact: Dr. Larry Gianchetla, Dean, School of Business Administration, University of Montana, Missoula, MT 59812; Telephone: 406-243-6195.

INDIVIDUAL COURSES

The University of Montana offers individual for-credit courses in: accounting (graduate); public administration (graduate); teacher education (graduate).

UNIVERSITY OF NEBRASKA–LINCOLN
LINCOLN, NE 68588

The University of Nebraska–Lincoln first offered a degree program via distance education in 1986.

Total enrollment in distance education programs (1992–93): 189.

Number graduating from distance programs (spring 1992): 2.

Nebraska CorpNet is a training network for the on-site delivery of University of Nebraska–Lincoln college courses and workshops. The CorpNet system broadcasts live, on-campus classes utilizing one-way video and two-way audio connections. CorpNet utilizes Instructional Television Fixed Service (ITFS) and compressed satellite signals to deliver graduate programs and noncredit seminars to 17 corporate sites and 8 public sites across Nebraska.

DEGREE PROGRAMS

INDUSTRIAL AND MANAGEMENT SYSTEMS ENGINEERING
Nebraska CorpNet. Master's degree program covering systems management, operations research, human factors, manufacturing, and processes.

Requirements: Same as for on-campus graduate students.

Degree/Certificate Awarded: Master's—M.S.I.E.

Availability: Open to the public; statewide.

Primary Methods of Course Delivery and Response: Compressed-video television; electronic mail; satellite television; teleconferencing.

Accreditation: Accreditation Board for Engineering and Technology.

For more information, contact: Nancy Aden, Division of Continuing Studies, University of Nebraska–Lincoln, 157 Nebraska Center, Lincoln, NE 68583-0900; Telephone: 402-472-1924; Fax: 402-472-1901; Internet: naden@unl.edu.

MANUFACTURING SYSTEMS ENGINEERING
Nebraska CorpNet. An interdisciplinary master's degree in electrical, industrial, and mechanical engineering and the college of business administration.

Requirements: Same as for on-campus graduate students.

Degree/Certificate Awarded: Master's—M.S., M.S.E.

Availability: Open to the public; statewide.

Primary Methods of Course Delivery and Response: Compressed-video television; electronic mail; satellite television; teleconferencing.

Accreditation: Accreditation Board for Engineering and Technology.

For more information, contact: Nancy Aden, Division of Continuing Studies, University of Nebraska–Lincoln, 157 Nebraska Center, Lincoln, NE 68583-0900; Telephone: 402-472-1924; Fax: 402-472-1901; Internet: naden@unl.edu.

BUSINESS ADMINISTRATION
Nebraska CorpNet. A non-thesis master's degree program including course work from accounting, finance, economics, management, and marketing.

Requirements: Same as for on-campus graduate students.

Degree/Certificate Awarded: Master's—M.B.A.

Availability: Open to the public; local—Scottsbluff and Offutt Air Force Base.

Primary Methods of Course Delivery and Response: Compressed-video television; electronic mail; satellite television; teleconferencing.

Accreditation: American Assembly of Collegiate Schools of Business.

For more information, contact: Nancy Aden, Division of Continuing Studies, University of Nebraska–Lincoln, 157 Nebraska Center, Lincoln, NE 68583-0900; Telephone: 402-472-1924; Fax: 402-472-1901; Internet: naden@unl.edu.

COMPUTER SCIENCE
Nebraska CorpNet. Master's program in computer science offers course work in theory of computation, algorithms, hardware and architecture, software, and applications.

Requirements: Same as for on-campus graduate students.

Degree/Certificate Awarded: Master's—M.S.C.S.

Availability: Open to the public; statewide.

Primary Methods of Course Delivery and Response: Compressed-video television; electronic mail; satellite television; teleconferencing.

For more information, contact: Nancy Aden, Division of Continuing Studies, University of Nebraska–Lincoln, 157 Nebraska Center, Lincoln, NE 68583-0900; Telephone: 402-472-1924; Fax: 402-472-1901; Internet: naden@unl.edu.

MECHANICAL ENGINEERING
Nebraska CorpNet. Master's program in mechanical engineering includes thermal/fluid sciences, systems and design, and metallurgical and materials engineering.

Requirements: Same as for on-campus graduate students.

Degree/Certificate Awarded: Master's—M.S.M.E.

Availability: Open to the public; statewide.

Primary Methods of Course Delivery and Response: Compressed-video television; electronic mail; satellite television; teleconferencing.

Accreditation: Accreditation Board for Engineering and Technology.

For more information, contact: Nancy Aden, Division of Continuing Studies, University of Nebraska–Lincoln, 157 Nebraska Center, Lincoln, NE 68583-0900; Telephone: 402-472-1924; Fax: 402-472-1901; Internet: naden@unl.edu.

INDIVIDUAL COURSES

The University of Nebraska–Lincoln offers individual for-credit courses in:

business/management (undergraduate and graduate); computer science (undergraduate and graduate); engineering (undergraduate and graduate); teacher education (graduate).

UNIVERSITY OF NEW BRUNSWICK

FREDERICTON, NEW BRUNSWICK E3B 5A3, CANADA

The University of New Brunswick first offered a degree program via distance
education in 1982.
Total enrollment in distance education programs (1992–93): 600.

Number graduating from distance programs (spring 1992): 20.

DEGREE PROGRAMS

EDUCATION
M.A. in Education. Supervisory program leading to principalship; advanced
teacher education.

Requirements: Bachelor's degree.

Degree/Certificate Awarded: Master's—M.A.

Availability: Open to the public; provincewide.

Primary Methods of Course Delivery and Response: Teleconferencing;
videoconferencing (secondary means).

On-Campus Component: One summer session.

Accreditation: Nurses Association of New Brunswick.

For more information, contact: Dr. John Morris, Director, Extension and Summer
Session, University of New Brunswick, P.O. Box 4400, Fredericton, New Brunswick
E3B 5A3, Canada; Telephone: 506-453-4646; Fax: 506-453-3572.

TEACHER EDUCATION
B.A. in Education.

Requirements: Completion of one university for-credit course or high school
diploma.

Degree/Certificate Awarded: Bachelor's—B.A.

Availability: Open to the public; provincewide.

Primary Methods of Course Delivery and Response: Cable television; public television;
teleconferencing.

On-Campus Component: Two summer sessions.

Accreditation: Nurses Association of New Brunswick.

For more information, contact: Dr. John Morris, Director, Extension and Summer
Session, University of New Brunswick, P.O. Box 4400, Fredericton, New Brunswick
E3B 5A3, Canada; Telephone: 506-453-4646; Fax: 506-453-3572.

NURSING
B.S. in Nursing.

Requirements: Successful completion of diploma program for RNs; one year of
clinical experience in nursing.

Degree/Certificate Awarded: Bachelor's—B.S.

Availability: Open to RNs; national; also available to Bermuda residents.

Primary Methods of Course Delivery and Response: Audiocassette; compressed-video television; public television; teleconferencing.

Accreditation: Nurses Association of New Brunswick.

For more information, contact: Dr. John Morris, Director, Extension and Summer Session, University of New Brunswick, P.O. Box 4400, Fredericton, New Brunswick E3B 5A3, Canada; Telephone: 506-453-4646; Fax: 506-453-3572.

INDIVIDUAL COURSES

The University of New Brunswick offers individual for-credit courses in: accounting (undergraduate); business/management (undergraduate and graduate); liberal arts/general studies (undergraduate); nursing (undergraduate and graduate); teacher education (undergraduate and graduate).

UNIVERSITY OF NORTH CAROLINA AT GREENSBORO
GREENSBORO, NC 27412-5001

Total enrollment in distance education programs (1992–93): 60.

At the University of North Carolina at Greensboro, library science courses are taught to regular on-campus students and either videotaped or televised; tapes are then sent to several sites in Virginia or televised over the MCNC network. The school is currently considering offering the full degree to students in Virginia.

DEGREE PROGRAM

LIBRARY SCIENCE
LIS-Virginia. Courses leading to a graduate degree in library science. Primarily lecture.

Requirements: Bachelor's degree.

Degree/Certificate Awarded: None at this time; not yet approved.

Availability: Open to the public; specific sites in Virginia.

Primary Methods of Course Delivery and Response: Satellite television; videocassette.

On-Campus Component: Two summer sessions.

For more information, contact: Dr. Marilyn Miller, Head of Library and Information Studies, School of Education, University of North Carolina at Greensboro, Curry Building, Greensboro, NC 27412; Telephone: 919-334-5100.

INDIVIDUAL COURSES

The University of North Carolina at Greensboro offers an individual for-credit course in: library science (graduate).

UNIVERSITY OF NORTH DAKOTA
GRAND FORKS, ND 58202

The University of North Dakota first offered a degree program via distance education in 1985.

Total enrollment in distance education programs (1992–93): 179.

Number graduating from distance programs (spring 1992): 5.

The University of North Dakota has been providing degree programs via interactive television, an educational network, a public television network, and videotape for several years. The interactive network connects all 11 public postsecondary institutions in the state. As of fall 1993, the University of North Dakota will also offer courses via satellite uplink.

DEGREE PROGRAMS

NURSING
Undergraduate Nursing Program. Basic curriculum.

Requirements: Same as for on-campus students.

Degree/Certificate Awarded: Bachelor's—B.S.N.

Availability: Open to admitted students only; statewide.

Primary Methods of Course Delivery and Response: Compressed-video television; fax; telephone.

On-Campus Component: From 2 to 12 weeks.

Accreditation: National League for Nursing, North Dakota State Board of Nursing.

For more information, contact: Dr. Judith Euller, Director of Undergraduate Distance Education, College of Nursing, University of North Dakota, Box 9025, Grand Forks, ND 58202; Telephone: 701-777-4508; Fax: 701-777-4096.

MEDICAL TECHNOLOGY
Distant Learning Program in Medical Technology. Essentially the same curriculum offered on campus.

Requirements: Same as for on-campus students.

Degree/Certificate Awarded: Bachelor's—B.S.M.T.

Availability: Open to the public; regional—Montana, South Dakota, Wyoming, Minnesota, and North Dakota.

Primary Methods of Course Delivery and Response: Fax; teleconferencing; telephone.

On-Campus Component: Five weeks for various lab work.

Accreditation: National Accrediting Agency for Clinical Laboratory Sciences.

For more information, contact: Judy Newell, Coordinator, Distance Learning, Medical Technology, University of North Dakota, Box 8277, Grand Forks, ND, 58202; Telephone: 701-777-2651; Fax: 701-772-9636.

PUBLIC ADMINISTRATION
Master's in Public Administration. A generalist orientation to prepare students for a career in public and nonprofit management and policy.

Requirements: 2.75 overall GPA or 3.0 for the last two years of undergraduate work; GMAT or GRE; 20 credits of prerequisites in political science management, accounting, or statistics.

Degree/Certificate Awarded: Master's—M.P.A.

Availability: Open to the public; local; currently limited to one distant site.

Primary Methods of Course Delivery and Response: Compressed-video television; fax; telephone.

For more information, contact: Don Cozzetto, Director of Graduate Studies, Political Science, University of North Dakota, Box 8379, Grand Forks, ND 58202; Telephone: 701-777-3831; Fax: 701-777-5099.

BUSINESS ADMINISTRATION
Master of Business Administration. Seeks to develop knowledge of basic business functions, decision-making skills, and understanding of how internal and external factors affect the management of organizations.

Requirements: Bachelor's degree from accredited college or university; 2.75 overall GPA or 3.0 for the last two years of undergraduate work; 450 GMAT.

Degree/Certificate Awarded: Master's—M.B.A.

Availability: Open to the public; local; currently limited to one distant site.

Primary Methods of Course Delivery and Response: Compressed-video television; fax; telephone.

Accreditation: American Assembly of Collegiate Schools of Business.

For more information, contact: Eric Giltner, M.B.A. Program Administrator, Business Administration, University of North Dakota, Box 8098, Grand Forks, ND 58202; Telephone: 701-777-2135; Fax: 701-777-5099.

COUNSELING
Chemical Use/Abuse Interdisciplinary Minor. Completion of academic courses that constitute this minor is one step in securing a license as an addiction counselor in North Dakota.

Requirements: Bachelor's degree in social work or master's in counseling.

Degree/Certificate Awarded: Postsecondary certificate.

Availability: Open to the public; statewide; five distant sites.

Primary Methods of Course Delivery and Response: Compressed-video television; fax; telephone.

Accreditation: Council for Social Work Education.

For more information, contact: Thomasine Heitcamp, Associate Professor, Social Work, University of North Dakota, Box 7090, Grand Forks, ND 58202; Telephone: 701-777-2877; Fax: 701-777-3650.

SOCIAL WORK
Bachelor's Degree in Social Work. Basic undergraduate curriculum.

Requirements: Same as for on-campus students.

Degree/Certificate Awarded: Bachelor's—B.S.W.

Availability: Open to the public; statewide; four distant sites.

Primary Methods of Course Delivery and Response: Compressed-video television; fax; telephone.

Accreditation: Council for Social Work Education.

For more information, contact: Thomasine Heitcamp, Associate Professor, Social Work, University of North Dakota, Box 7090, Grand Forks, ND 58202; Telephone: 701-777-2877; Fax: 701-777-3650.

EDUCATION
Education Specialist Degree. Specialist diploma (64 semester hours beyond the bachelor's degree). A terminal program of advanced preparation for professional practice in educational administration. Curriculum is the same as on campus.

Requirements: Same as for on-campus students.

Degree/Certificate Awarded: Ed.S.

Availability: Open to the public; local; two distant sites.

Primary Methods of Course Delivery and Response: Compressed-video television; fax; telephone.

On-Campus Component: One semester of full-time enrollment at the University of North Dakota campus.

Accreditation: National Council for Accreditation of Teacher Education.

For more information, contact: Don Lemon, Professor and Chair, Educational Administration, University of North Dakota, Box 7189, Grand Forks, ND 58202; Telephone: 701-777-4255; Fax: 701-777-4365.

ENGINEERING
Corporate Engineering Degree Program. Bachelor of Science degrees in chemical, electrical, and mechanical engineering.

Requirements: Same as for on-campus students.

Degree/Certificate Awarded: Bachelor's—B.S.E.E., B.S.M.E., B.S.C.H.E.

Consortium Affiliation: Corporate Engineering Degree Program Consortium members: University of North Dakota, 3M, DuPont, Hutchinson Technology, and GE Plastics.

Availability: Open to consortium members only; national.

Primary Methods of Course Delivery and Response: Fax; telephone; videocassette.

On-Campus Component: Not yet determined.

Accreditation: Accreditation Board for Engineering and Technology.

For more information, contact: Clyde Eisenbeis, Assistant to the Dean, School of Engineering and Mines, University of North Dakota, Box 8155, Grand Forks, ND 58202; Telephone: 701-777-3875; Fax: 701-777-4838.

INDIVIDUAL COURSES

The University of North Dakota offers individual for-credit courses in: allied health (undergraduate); liberal arts/general studies (undergraduate); social work (undergraduate); teacher education (graduate).

PATRICIA SJOLIE

Age: 34

Home: Fergus Falls, Minnesota

Institution: University of North Dakota

Courses taken: Via distance learning speaker phone: hematology, parasitology, microbiology, immunohematology, quality assurance. Via cable television: philosophy, history. Other electives taken via correspondence courses.

Academic goals: In May 1993, Sjolie received her B.S. degree in medical technology. She also holds a two-year medical technician degree from Fergus Falls Community College.

"I was working as a medical lab technician (MLT) at Lake Region Hospital. I had my two-year degree, but in order to be a section supervisor you must have a B.S. degree. The head of the MLT program at Fergus Falls Community College heard about the University of North Dakota's distance learning program and asked the MLTs if we'd be interested. We knew that distance learning was the only way we could earn our B.S. degrees, work full time, and live in Fergus Falls. So five of us began this program in December 1989.

"The hardest part was probably the beginning. We had to talk one of the chemistry teachers at the community college into teaching the upper-level course—otherwise we would have had to take off work for a semester and attend the University of North Dakota campus two hours away. Instead of paying for the course by credit hour, the community college figured out what the expenses would be, and we found other students to take the class so [the cost] was divided by the number of students. It was considerably more than the per-credit cost, but it was worth it to be able to take the class locally—even though for five months it meant working from 7 A.M. to 3:30 P.M., attending class three nights a week from 6 to 10 P.M., and studying until 1 A.M.!

"But after that, most of the courses were by speaker phone. The quality was very good. We could hear the professors and the students' questions. We would have to take off from work and drive to UND for the labs. Lab time amounted to three two-week sessions and one one-week session, but the hospital was supportive and gave us the time off for labs.

"We also had to listen to 90 hours of audiotapes of lectures from around the country. The tapes were mailed to us periodically, and we were tested on their subject matter.

"One elective I really liked was philosophy, which was broadcast on Prairie Public Television. It aired on Saturday mornings, but I would tape it and watch it later. A panel of experts discussed the subject at hand, we had a syllabus from UND to follow, and we answered the questions and returned them to UND.

"Four of my original class of five have graduated. I have young children who now know what it's like to have a mother who isn't always studying. At work I am now education coordinator for the MLT interns."

Sjoile is a medical technology generalist at Lake Region Hospital.

UNIVERSITY OF SOUTH CAROLINA
COLUMBIA, SC 29208

The University of South Carolina first offered a degree program via distance education in 1969.

Total enrollment in distance education programs (1992–93): 4,000.

Number graduating from distance programs (spring 1992): 65.

The University of South Carolina uses a statewide ITFS system (converting in 1994 to digital satellite) with interactive audio and videocassette to deliver complete master's programs as well as core master's-level courses. The school offers substantial student services to support distant learners.

DEGREE PROGRAMS

LIBRARY AND INFORMATION SCIENCE

Master of Library and Information Science. A 36-semester-hours program with specializations in public, academic, school, and special libraries and other information agencies.

Requirements: 950 GRE (verbal and quantitative) or 50 MAT; 3.0 GPR; 550 TOEFL.

Degree/Certificate Awarded: Master's—M.L.I.S.

Availability: Open to the public; currently in South Carolina, West Virginia, and Georgia only.

Primary Methods of Course Delivery and Response: Electronic mail; fax; interactive audio; satellite television; telephone.

Accreditation: American Library Association, National Association of State Directors of Teacher Education and Certification/National Council for Accreditation of Teacher Education.

For more information, contact: Gayle D. Sykes, Assistant Dean, College of Library and Information Science, University of South Carolina, Columbia, SC 29208; Telephone: 803-777-3858; Fax: 803-777-7938; Internet: ILIBS16@UNIVSCVM.CSD.SCAROLINA.EDU; Bitnet: ILIBS16@UNIVSCUM.

ENGINEERING

APOGEE. Master of Engineering and Master of Science degrees in chemical engineering, civil engineering, mechanical engineering, electrical engineering, and computer engineering.

Requirements: Vary by department.

Degree/Certificate Awarded: Master's—M.E., M.S.

Consortium Affiliation: Some courses used in the NTU program (Fort Collins, CO).

Availability: Open to engineers; regional.

Primary Methods of Course Delivery and Response: Closed-circuit television; interactive audio; videocassette.

On-Campus Component: 90 minutes per course on four Saturdays each semester.

For more information, contact: Phyllis Coleman, APOGEE Director, College of Engineering, University of South Carolina, Columbia, SC 29208; Telephone: 803-777-4192; Fax: 803-777-9597.

BUSINESS
Professional Master of Business Administration. Fully accredited M.B.A. program for working professionals.

Requirements: Undergraduate degree; GMAT; two years' work experience.

Degree/Certificate Awarded: Master's—M.B.A.

Availability: Open to the public; statewide.

Primary Methods of Course Delivery and Response: Closed-circuit television; interactive audio.

On-Campus Component: 15 Saturday sessions a year.

Accreditation: American Assembly of Collegiate Schools of Business.

For more information, contact: Paul Yazel, Assistant Director of M.B.A. Programs, College of Business Administration, University of South Carolina, Columbia, SC 29208; Telephone: 803-777-7940; Fax: 803-777-9018.

INDIVIDUAL COURSES

The University of South Carolina offers individual for-credit courses in: business/management (graduate); criminal justice/law (undergraduate and graduate); engineering (undergraduate and graduate); liberal arts/general studies (undergraduate and graduate); library and information science (undergraduate and graduate); nursing (undergraduate and graduate); public health (undergraduate and graduate); social work (graduate); teacher education (undergraduate and graduate).

UNIVERSITY OF TENNESSEE, KNOXVILLE
KNOXVILLE, TN 37996

The University of Tennessee, Knoxville, first offered a degree program via distance education in 1975.
Total enrollment in distance education programs (1992–93): 4,000.
Number graduating from distance programs (spring 1992): 12.

The University of Tennessee, Knoxville, offers traditional undergraduate and graduate correspondence courses and selected graduate engineering programs via videotape and interactive video courses through its main campus and through three centers in Tullahoma, Kingsport, and Oak Ridge.

DEGREE PROGRAMS

ENGINEERING MANAGEMENT
Principles of management for application in industrial settings.

Requirements: Bachelor's degree in engineering or science; two years work experience in engineering or science.

Degree/Certificate Awarded: Master's—M.S.

Availability: Open to the public; national.

Primary Methods of Course Delivery and Response: Videocassette.

For more information, contact: Hal Schmitt, Director, Industrial Development Programming, University of Tennessee, Knoxville, 419 Conference Center Bldg., Knoxville, TN 37996; Telephone: 615-974-0236; Fax: 615-974-0264; Internet: PA145128@UTKVMI.

ENGINEERING
UTSI College of Engineering Graduate Program Master of Science in Engineering. Includes aerospace, chemical, electrical and computer, science and mechanics, industrial, and mechanical engineering, engineering management, mathematics, and physics.

Requirements: B.S. from an accredited college with 2.5 GPA or 3.0 in senior year.

Degree/Certificate Awarded: Master's—M.S.

Availability: Open to the public; national.

Primary Method of Course Delivery and Response: Videocassette.

On-Campus Component: Students attend some classes on site.

For more information, contact: Penny Smith, Administrative Assistant, University of Tennessee Space Institute, B. H. Goethert Rd., Tullahoma, TN 37388; Telephone: 615-393-7293; Bitnet: MSMITH1@UTSIV1.

ENGINEERING

Oak Ridge Resident Graduate Program Master of Science in Engineering. Includes chemical, electrical, environmental, industrial, and nuclear engineering.

Requirements: B.S. in engineering with 2.5 GPA or 3.0 in senior year.

Degree/Certificate Awarded: Master's—M.S.

Availability: Open to Department of Engineering, DOE contractors, and residents of Oak Ridge; local.

Primary Methods of Course Delivery and Response: Interactive videodisc; videocassette.

On-Campus Component: Students attend classes at Oak Ridge Center for on-site or interactive classes; video available for individual use.

For more information, contact: Joan Howell, Coordinator, Oak Ridge Resident Graduate Program, P.O. Box 117, Oak Ridge, TN 37831-0117; Telephone: 615-376-3429; Bitnet: PB123788@UTKVM1.

ENGINEERING

Kingsport University Center Master of Science in Engineering. Chemical, civil, industrial, mechanical, and electrical and computer engineering offered through a combination of video, interactive video, and on-site instruction.

Requirements: B.S. in engineering with 2.5 GPA or 3.0 in senior year.

Degree/Certificate Awarded: Master's—M.S.

Availability: Open to the public; local.

Primary Methods of Course Delivery and Response: Interactive videodisc; videocassette.

On-Campus Component: Students attend classes at Kingsport Center or individual company locations.

For more information, contact: Lois Presley, Coordinator, University of Tennessee Kingsport University Center, University Blvd., Kingsport, TN 37660; Telephone: 615-392-8040; Fax: 615-392-8014; Bitnet: PA159328@UTKUM1.

INDIVIDUAL COURSES

The University of Tennessee offers individual for-credit courses in: accounting (undergraduate); agriculture (undergraduate); business/management (undergraduate); criminal justice/law (undergraduate and graduate); engineering (undergraduate and graduate); environmental health and safety (undergraduate); foreign languages (undergraduate); liberal arts/general studies (undergraduate); teacher education (undergraduate and graduate).

UNIVERSITY OF VIRGINIA
CHARLOTTESVILLE, VA 22903

The University of Virginia first offered a degree program via distance education in 1983.

Total enrollment in distance education programs (1992–93): 1,000.

Number graduating from distance programs (spring 1992): 30.

The University of Virginia's advanced communication systems enable the Division of Continuing Education to originate, transmit, and receive interactive instructional programs statewide and nationwide.

DEGREE PROGRAMS

ENGINEERING

Virginia Commonwealth Graduate Engineering Program. Graduate programs in chemical, civil, electrical, materials science, mechanical and aerospace, nuclear, and systems engineering.

Requirements: Four-year undergraduate degree, usually in engineering.

Degree/Certificate Awarded: Master's—M.E.

Consortium Affiliation: Virginia Cooperative Engineering Program.

Availability: Open to the public; national.

Primary Method of Course Delivery and Response: Satellite television.

For more information, contact: Dr. George Cahen, Assistant Dean for Graduate Programs, Engineering and Applied Science, University of Virginia, Thornton Hall, Charlottesville, VA 22903; Telephone: 804-982-5781.

INDIVIDUAL COURSES

The University of Virginia offers an individual for-credit course in: teacher education (graduate).

UNIVERSITY OF WISCONSIN–MADISON
MADISON, WI 53706

The University of Wisconsin–Madison first offered a degree program via distance education in 1987.
Total enrollment in distance education programs (1992–93): 1,137.

Number graduating from distance programs (spring 1992): 4.

The University of Wisconsin–Madison offers credit and non-credit courses via cable TV, videotape, audiographics, and satellite. The College of Engineering is a member of the National Technological University and is a pioneer in the use of audiographics for distance education.

DEGREE PROGRAMS

NUCLEAR ENGINEERING
Engineering Outreach.

Requirements: 2.75 GPA.

Degree/Certificate Awarded: Master's—M.S.N.E.E.P.

Consortium Affiliation: National Technological University.

Availability: Open to the public; national.

Primary Methods of Course Delivery and Response: Satellite television; videocassette.

On-Campus Component: Three-week summer intersession laboratory course.

For more information, contact: Helene Demont, Program Assistant, Engineering Outreach, University of Wisconsin–Madison, 1415 Johnson Drive, Room 2713, Madison, WI 53706-1691; Telephone: 608-262-5516; Fax: 608-262-6400; Internet: demont@engr.wisc.edu.

POWER ELECTRONICS
Engineering Outreach.

Requirements: 2.75 GPA.

Degree/Certificate Awarded: Master's—M.S.E.E.

Consortium Affiliation: National Technological University.

Availability: Open to the public; national.

Primary Methods of Course Delivery and Response: Satellite television; videocassette.

On-Campus Component: Three-week summer intersession laboratory course.

For more information, contact: Helene Demont, Program Assistant, Engineering Outreach, University of Wisconsin–Madison, 1415 Johnson Drive, Room 2713, Madison, WI 53706-1691; Telephone: 608-262-5516; Fax: 608-262-6400; Internet: demont@engr.wisc.edu.

CONTROLS
Engineering Outreach.

Requirements: 2.75 GPA.

Degree/Certificate Awarded: Master's—M.S.M.E.

Consortium Affiliation: National Technological University.

Availability: Open to the public; national.

Primary Methods of Course Delivery and Response: Satellite television; videocassette.

On-Campus Component: Three-week summer intersession laboratory course.

For more information, contact: Helene Demont, Program Assistant, Engineering Outreach, University of Wisconsin–Madison, 1415 Johnson Drive, Room 2713, Madison, WI 53706-1691; Telephone: 608-262-5516; Fax: 608-262-6400; Internet: demont@engr.wisc.edu.

INDIVIDUAL COURSES

The University of Wisconsin–Madison offers individual for-credit courses in: business/management (undergraduate); engineering (undergraduate and graduate); food science (undergraduate); liberal arts/general studies (undergraduate); nursing (undergraduate); social work (undergraduate and graduate); teacher education (undergraduate and graduate).

UNIVERSITY OF WYOMING
LARAMIE, WY 82071

The University of Wyoming first offered a degree program via distance education in 1984.

Total enrollment in distance education programs (1992–93): 521.

Number graduating from distance programs (spring 1992): 50.

DEGREE PROGRAMS

SOCIAL SCIENCE
Plan V—Bachelor's Degree in Social Science. Major is distributed across the social sciences.

Requirements: Same as for on-campus students.

Degree/Certificate Awarded: Bachelor's—B.S.

Availability: Open to the public; regional.

Primary Methods of Course Delivery and Response: Telephone; videocassette.

For more information, contact: Charlotte Farr, Coordinator, Office of Off-Campus Credit Courses, University of Wyoming, Box 3106, University Station, Laramie, WY 82071; Telephone: 307-766-5645; Fax: 307-766-3445; Internet: CWFARR@CORRAL.UWYO.EDU.

PUBLIC ADMINISTRATION
Master's in Public Administration. Designed for public servants from diverse backgrounds, the program covers political, legal, economic, social, organizational, and managerial concepts.

Requirements: 900 composite verbal/quantitative score on GRE; 3.0 GPA.

Degree/Certificate Awarded: Master's—M.P.A.

Availability: Open to the public; regional.

Primary Methods of Course Delivery and Response: telephone; videocassette.

On-Campus Component: Periodic weekend classes at a central location.

For more information, contact: Charlotte Farr, Coordinator, Office of Off-Campus Credit Courses, University of Wyoming, Box 3106, University Station, Laramie, WY 82071; Telephone: 307-766-5645; Fax: 307-766-3445; Internet: CWFARR@CORRAL.UWYO.EDU.

ADULT EDUCATION
Master's in Adult Education. Lifelong learning issues including the adult learner, programs and practices, and teaching adults.

Requirements: 900 composite verbal/quantitative score on GRE; 3.0 GPA.

Degree/Certificate Awarded: Master's—M.A.

Availability: Open to the public; regional.

Primary Methods of Course Delivery and Response: Telephone; videocassette.

On-Campus Component: One summer. Some courses also require one weekend in a central location.

For more information, contact: Charlotte Farr, Coordinator, Office of Off-Campus Credit Courses, University of Wyoming, Box 3106, University Station, Laramie, WY 82071; Telephone: 307-766-5645; Fax: 307-766-3445; Internet: CWFARR@CORRAL.UWYO.EDU.

SPEECH PATHOLOGY
Master's in Speech Pathology. Covers curriculum recommended for public school certification.

Requirements: 3.25 GPA; above 25th percentile on GRE.

Degree/Certificate Awarded: Master's—M.S.

Availability: Open to the public; national.

Primary Methods of Course Delivery and Response: Telephone; videocassette.

On-Campus Component: At least two summers.

For more information, contact: Charlotte Farr, Coordinator, Office of Off-Campus Credit Courses, University of Wyoming, Box 3106, University Station, Laramie, WY 82071; Telephone: 307-766-5645; Fax: 307-766-3445; Internet: CWFARR@CORRAL.UWYO.EDU.

INDIVIDUAL COURSES

The University of Wyoming offers individual for-credit courses in: business/management (undergraduate); criminal justice/law (undergraduate); engineering (undergraduate); liberal arts/general studies (undergraduate); social work (undergraduate); teacher education (undergraduate).

UTAH STATE UNIVERSITY
LOGAN, UT 84322

Utah State University first offered a degree program via distance education in 1984.
Total enrollment in distance education programs (1992–93): 3,760.

Utah State University offers COM-NET, an electronic distance learning system. In the classroom, instructors have immediate access to all course participants through a fully interactive audio teleconferencing system. Using slow-scanned still-frame video, students can see overheads, photographs, charts, and other visual materials. On-site technical assistants provide support for instructors and students by acting as classroom facilitators, test proctors, and equipment technicians. COM-NET delivers courses to Utah State University outreach centers located throughout Utah. These outreach centers provide a full range of student services, such as registration, text and syllabi distribution, and access to library resources.

DEGREE PROGRAMS

PSYCHOLOGY
Bachelor's degree completion program. Prepares students for employment or acceptance into graduate programs.

Requirements: Application; GPA and entrance test scores.

Degree/Certificate Awarded: Bachelor's—B.S.

Availability: Open to the public; statewide.

Primary Methods of Course Delivery and Response: Closed-circuit television; commercial television; compressed-video television; electronic writing board; fax; telephone.

For more information, contact: Louis D. Griffin, Director, Electronic Distance Education, Life Span Learning, Utah State University, Logan, UT 84322-3720; Telephone: 801-750-2028; Fax: 801-750-1399.

HUMAN RESOURCE MANAGEMENT
An interdisciplinary degree covering human resource planning, recruiting, selection, placement, benefits, performance management, career planning, training and development, labor relations, and ethical/legal employment practices.

Requirements: Application; three letters of recommendation; GRE or GMAT.

Degree/Certificate Awarded: Master's—M.S.

Availability: Open to the public; statewide.

Primary Methods of Course Delivery and Response: Closed-circuit television; commercial television; compressed-video television; fax; telephone.

For more information, contact: Louis D. Griffin, Director, Electronic Distance

Education, Life Span Learning, Utah State University, Logan, UT 84322-3720; Telephone: 801-750-2028; Fax: 801-750-1399.

SCHOOL COUNSELING
Master's degree program.

Requirements: Application; appropriate undergraduate degree; GRE scores.

Degree/Certificate Awarded: Master's—M.S.

Availability: Open to the public; statewide.

Primary Methods of Course Delivery and Response: Closed-circuit television; commercial television; compressed-video television; electronic writing board; fax; telephone.

For more information, contact: Louis D. Griffin, Director, Electronic Distance Education, Life Span Learning, Utah State University, Logan, UT 84322-3720; Telephone: 801-750-2028; Fax: 801-750-1399.

BUSINESS ADMINISTRATION
Bachelor's degree completion program. Course work covers all major business functions.

Requirements: Must be in good standing with the university. Transfer students must have a 2.2 GPA.

Degree/Certificate Awarded: Bachelor's—B.S.

Availability: Open to the public; statewide.

Primary Methods of Course Delivery and Response: Closed-circuit television; commercial television; compressed-video television; electronic writing board; fax; telephone.

For more information, contact: Louis D. Griffin, Director, Electronic Distance Education, Life Span Learning, Utah State University, Logan, UT 84322-3720; Telephone: 801-750-2028; Fax: 801-750-1399.

INDIVIDUAL COURSES

Utah State University offers individual for-credit courses in: accounting (undergraduate); business/management (undergraduate and graduate); computer science (undergraduate); engineering (undergraduate); environmental health and safety (undergraduate); liberal arts/general studies (undergraduate and graduate); social work (undergraduate); teacher education (undergraduate and graduate).

VIRGINIA POLYTECHNIC INSTITUTE AND STATE UNIVERSITY
BLACKSBURG, VA 24061-0202

Virginia Polytechnic Institute and State University first offered a degree program via distance education in 1983.

Total enrollment in distance education programs (1992–93): 1,374.

Number graduating from distance programs (spring 1992): 103.

Virginia Polytechnic Institute and State University's distance-education program is integrated with four other state institutions and features one-way satellite video and two-way audio using a telephone bridging network. Instructors teach "live" classes on campus, and they are extended via satellite.

DEGREE PROGRAM

ENGINEERING
Virginia Cooperative Graduate Engineering Program. Virginia Tech teaches eight courses each semester via statewide satellite (G-2) network.

Requirements: Same as for on-campus graduate study except that students can register for one course while application materials are being processed.

Degree/Certificate Awarded: Master's—M.S. or M.E., electrical, mechanical, systems, civil, or industrial engineering.

Consortium Affiliation: Virginia Cooperative Graduate Engineering Program, Virginia State Council of Higher Education, Richmond, VA.

Availability: Open to the public; national (but statewide emphasis).

Primary Methods of Course Delivery and Response: two-way audio telephone; satellite television.

For more information, contact: Benjamin S. Blanchard, Assistant Dean, College of Engineering, 333 Norris Hall, Virginia Polytechnic Institute and State University, Blacksburg, VA 24061; Telephone: 703-231-5458; Fax: 703-231-7248.

INDIVIDUAL COURSES

Virginia Polytechnic Institute and State University offers an individual for-credit course in: engineering (graduate).

WASHINGTON STATE UNIVERSITY
PULLMAN, WA 99164

Washington State University first offered a degree program via distance education in 1974.
Total enrollment in distance education programs (1992–93): 3,000.

A bachelor's degree in social sciences is offered through Washington State University's Extended Degree Program. Upper-division courses leading to the degree are offered solely via distance technologies, including satellite, videotape, and correspondence study (and, in the planning stages, computer conferencing). Washington State University also operates a fully interactive microwave telecommunications system that delivers courses to its three branch campuses (and is being expanded to other areas of the state). Courses delivered on this system supplement the degree programs at the branch campuses and at Pullman. Between 90 and 100 courses a year are currently offered on the system.

DEGREE PROGRAM

SOCIAL SCIENCES
B.A. in Social Sciences. Interdisciplinary liberal arts degree emphasizing anthropology, history, political science, and business.

Requirements: For transfer students, completion of 27 semester credits or 40 quarter credits with cumulative 2.0 GPA or better.

Degree/Certificate Awarded: Bachelor's—B.A.

Availability: Open to the public; national.

Primary Methods of Course Delivery and Response: Cable television; computer conferencing; fax; public television; satellite television.

For more information, contact: Janet Kendall, Associate Director, Extended Academic Programs, Washington State University, Pullman, WA 99164-5220; Telephone: 509-335-3557; Fax: 509-335-0945; Internet: KENDALLJ@WSUVM1.CSC. WSU.EDU; Bitnet: KENDALLJ@WSUVM1.

INDIVIDUAL COURSES

Washington State University offers individual for-credit courses in: business/management (undergraduate and graduate); computer science (undergraduate and graduate); engineering (undergraduate and graduate); food science (undergraduate and graduate); liberal arts/general studies (undergraduate and graduate); teacher education (undergraduate and graduate).

WESTERN MICHIGAN UNIVERSITY
KALAMAZOO, MI 49008

Western Michigan University first offered a degree program via distance education in 1992.
Total enrollment in distance education programs (1992–93): 138.

Western Michigan University's M.B.A. program allows students to interact live by satellite and two-way audio with a professor. Tapes can also be mailed to students for later viewing.

DEGREE PROGRAM

BUSINESS
Master of Business Administration–Michigan Information Technology Network (MITN). A 33-hour M.B.A. program via live interactive television and two-way audio.

Requirements: Undergraduate degree (may also require 30 hours of undergraduate prerequisites, some of which are offered via TV); graduate application; transcripts; $25 fee; GMAT.

Degree/Certificate Awarded: Master's—M.B.A.

Consortium Affiliation: MITN.

Availability: Open to the public; statewide.

Primary Methods of Course Delivery and Response: Satellite television; telephone; videocassette.

Accreditation: AACSB.

For more information, contact: Geraldine A. Schma, Director, Distance Education/Continuing Education, Western Michigan University, B-103 Ellsworth Hall, Kalamazoo, MI 49008; Telephone: 616-387-4198; Fax: 616-387-4222.

INDIVIDUAL COURSES

Western Michigan University offers an individual for-credit course in: business/management (graduate).

WEST VIRGINIA UNIVERSITY
MORGANTOWN, WV 26506

West Virginia University first offered a degree program via distance education in 1990.

Total enrollment in distance education programs (1992–93): 3,500.

Number graduating from distance programs (spring 1992): 339.

At West Virginia University, distance education electronic media credit courses are offered through SATNET–System Wide, which includes 16 public institutions throughout the state.

DEGREE PROGRAMS

NURSING
Bachelor of Science in Nursing; Master of Science in Nursing. The B.S.N. includes nursing courses for RNs; the M.S.N. consists of theory courses. Clinical courses are available by arrangement.

Requirements: Must be a high school graduate or diploma RN; SAT scores required of those who graduated in the last five years.

Degree/Certificate Awarded: Bachelor's—B.S.N., Master's—M.S.N.

Consortium Affiliation: Marshall University.

Availability: Open to the public; statewide.

Primary Methods of Course Delivery and Response: Satellite television; teleconferencing; telephone.

On-Campus Component: Clinical courses—depends on individual case.

For more information, contact: Dr. Jacqueline Riley, Assistant Dean, School of Nursing, West Virginia University, 1146 HSN, P.O. Box 9600, Morgantown, WV 26506; Telephone: 304-293-4831; Fax: 304-293-6836.

INDIVIDUAL COURSES

West Virginia University offers individual for-credit courses in: business/management (undergraduate and graduate); engineering (graduate); liberal arts/general studies (undergraduate); nursing (undergraduate); social work (graduate); teacher education (graduate).

WILFRID LAURIER UNIVERSITY
WATERLOO, ONTARIO N2L 3C5, CANADA

Wilfrid Laurier University first offered a degree program via distance education in 1978.
Total enrollment in distance education programs (1992–93): 2,579.
Number graduating from distance programs (spring 1992): 10.

Wilfrid Laurier University's distance education program serves over 1,000 students per term, representing ten countries. Programs combine an academically rigorous print package with videocassettes. The average completion rate is currently 84 percent.

DEGREE PROGRAM

SOCIOLOGY
General B.A. in Sociology. A 15-credit bachelor's program with a major in sociology.

Requirements: Grade 12 completion; age 21; two years work experience.

Degree/Certificate Awarded: Bachelor's—B.A.

Availability: Open to the public; national.

Primary Methods of Course Delivery and Response: Teleconferencing; videocassette.

For more information, contact: Cliff Bilyea, Director of Part-Time Studies, Wilfrid Laurier University, 75 University Ave., Waterloo, Ontario N2L 5N3, Canada; Telephone: 519-884-1970; Fax: 519-884-8829.

INDIVIDUAL COURSES

Wilfrid Laurier University offers individual for-credit courses in: accounting (undergraduate); business/management (undergraduate); criminal justice/law (undergraduate); liberal arts/general studies (undergraduate); social work (undergraduate).

GEOGRAPHIC INDEX

SUBJECT INDEX

THE ELECTRONIC UNIVERSITY

AERONAUTICS

Graduate Degree Programs
Embry-Riddle Aeronautical
University, 25

Undergraduate Degree Programs
Embry-Riddle Aeronautical
University, 25
See also AVIATION

AEROSPACE AND OCEAN ENGINEERING

Graduate Degree Programs
Florida Atlantic University, 27
Mary Washington College, 45
University of Alabama, 112
University of Colorado at
Boulder, 122
See also SPACE STUDIES

AGRICULTURAL ENGINEERING

Graduate Degree Programs
Colorado State University, 19

AGRICULTURE AND ANIMAL SCIENCES

Graduate Degree Programs
Iowa State University of Science and
Technology, 38

Undergraduate Degree Programs
Iowa State University of Science and
Technology, 38
Kansas State University, 41

Individual Courses
Iowa State University of Science and
Technology, 38
Kansas State University, 41
University of Kentucky, 137
University of Tennessee,
Knoxville, 159

ALLIED HEALTH

Individual Courses
Bastyr College, 5
Boise State University, 6
Chadron State College, 15
College of Great Falls, 16
Governors State University, 35
Mount Saint Vincent University, 46
Murray State University, 48
Northern Arizona University, 59

Old Dominion University, 63
Pennsylvania State University, 68
University of Alaska, Fairbanks, 114
University of Calgary, 119
University of Kentucky, 137
University of North Dakota, 153

ANIMAL SCIENCES. *SEE* AGRICULTURE AND ANIMAL SCIENCES

APPLIED ARTS AND SCIENCE

Undergraduate Degree Programs
Rochester Institute of
Technology, 82
See also INTERDISCIPLINARY
STUDIES; LIBERAL
ARTS/GENERAL STUDIES

APPLIED COMPUTING AND COMMUNICATIONS

Certificate Programs
Rochester Institute of
Technology, 82
See also COMPUTER SCIENCE

ARCHITECTURE AND ENVIRONMENTAL DESIGN

Individual Courses
Arizona State University, 2

ART. *SEE* ILLUSTRATION/ADVERTISING DESIGN

AUTOMATION. *SEE* ROBOTICS AND AUTOMATION

AVIATION

Undergraduate Degree Programs
Embry-Riddle Aeronautical
University, 25

Individual Courses
Embry-Riddle Aeronautical
University, 25
University of Alaska, Fairbanks, 114
See also AERONAUTICS

CHEMICAL ENGINEERING

Graduate Degree Programs

CHEMISTRY

Graduate Degree Programs

Individual Courses

CIVIL AND ENVIRONMENTAL ENGINEERING

Graduate Degree Programs

COMMUNICATIONS

Individual Courses

COMMUNITY MENTAL HEALTH

Individual Courses

COMPUTER SCIENCE

Graduate Degree Programs

Undergraduate Degree Programs

Certificate Programs

Individual Courses

**COMPUTER SCIENCE AND
ENGINEERING**

CONTINUING EDUCATION. *SEE*
ADULT AND CONTINUING
EDUCATION

CONTROLS

CORRECTIONAL ADMINISTRATION

COUNSELING

CRIMINAL JUSTICE/LAW

DATA COMMUNICATIONS

ENGINEERING; ENGINEERING
MANAGEMENT; INDUSTRIAL
AND MANAGEMENT SYSTEMS
ENGINEERING;
INTERDISCIPLINARY
ENGINEERING; MANAGEMENT
ENGINEERING;
MANUFACTURING SYSTEMS
ENGINEERING; MATERIALS
SCIENCE AND ENGINEERING;
MECHANICAL ENGINEERING;
MICROELECTRONICS
MANUFACTURING; MINING
ENGINEERING AND
TECHNOLOGY; NUCLEAR
ENGINEERING; OPTICAL
SCIENCES; POWER
ELECTRONICS; RELIABILITY
AND QUALITY ENGINEERING;
SOFTWARE ENGINEERING;
SYSTEMS ENGINEERING

ENGINEERING MANAGEMENT

Graduate Degree Programs
National Technological
University, 49
Old Dominion University, 63
Rensselaer Polytechnic Institute, 75
Southern Methodist University, 96
University of Colorado at
Boulder, 122
University of Missouri–Rolla, 144
University of Tennessee,
Knoxville, 159

ENGLISH

Individual Courses
University of Maryland University
College, 140

ENVIRONMENTAL DESIGN. *SEE*
ARCHITECTURE AND
ENVIRONMENTAL DESIGN

ENVIRONMENTAL ENGINEERING.
SEE CIVIL AND ENVIRONMENTAL
ENGINEERING

ENVIRONMENTAL HEALTH AND
SAFETY

Individual Courses
Corpus Christi State University, 23

Indiana State University, 37
Lehigh University, 43
Murray State University, 48
National Technological
University, 49
New Jersey Institute of
Technology, 54
Old Dominion University, 63
Oregon State University, 67
Rochester Institute of
Technology, 82
San Jose State University, 94
University of Colorado at
Boulder, 122
University of Colorado at Colorado
Springs, 128
University of Massachusetts at
Amherst, 143
University of Tennessee,
Knoxville, 159
Utah State University, 166
See also HEALTH PHYSICS

FAMILY STUDIES

Graduate Degree Programs
University of Kentucky, 137

Individual Courses
University of Kentucky, 137

FIRE PROTECTION
ADMINISTRATION AND
TECHNOLOGY

Undergraduate Degree Programs
California State University, Los
Angeles, 12

Individual Courses
California State University, Los
Angeles, 12
University of Maryland University
College, 140

FOOD SCIENCE

Undergraduate Degree Programs
Syracuse University, 105

Certificate Programs
Kansas State University, 41

Individual Courses
Syracuse University, 105
University of
Wisconsin–Madison, 162
Washington State University, 169

See also RESTAURANT AND FOOD SERVICE MANAGEMENT; TOURISM AND HOSPITALITY

FOREIGN LANGUAGES

Individual Courses
Boise State University, 6
Chadron State College, 15
College of Great Falls, 16
Murray State University, 48
National Technological University, 49
Thomas Edison State College, 111
University of Arizona, 116
University of Colorado at Colorado Springs, 128
University of Tennessee, Knoxville, 159

GENERAL SCIENCE. *SEE* SCIENCES

GENERAL STUDIES. *SEE* LIBERAL ARTS/GENERAL STUDIES

GEOGRAPHY

Individual Courses
Portland State University, 69

GERONTOLOGY

Certificate Programs
Mount Saint Vincent University, 46
See also LONG-TERM CARE ADMINISTRATION

GOVERNMENT

Individual Courses
University of Maryland University College, 140

GRAPHIC DESIGN. *SEE* ILLUSTRATION/ADVERTISING DESIGN

HAZARDOUS WASTE MANAGEMENT

Graduate Degree Programs
National Technological University, 49
See also ENVIRONMENTAL HEALTH AND SAFETY; HEALTH PHYSICS

HEALTH. *SEE* ALLIED HEALTH; COMMUNITY MENTAL HEALTH; ENVIRONMENTAL HEALTH AND SAFETY; GERONTOLOGY; MEDICAL TECHNOLOGY; NATURAL HEALTH AND NUTRITION; NURSING; PHARMACY; PROFESSIONAL ARTS; PUBLIC HEALTH; RADIOLOGIC TECHNOLOGY

HEALTH-CARE ADMINISTRATION

Graduate Degree Programs
Saint Joseph's College, 88

Undergraduate Degree Programs
Saint Joseph's College, 88

Certificate Programs
Rochester Institute of Technology, 82
Saint Joseph's College, 88

Individual Courses
Rochester Institute of Technology, 82
Saint Joseph's College, 88

HEALTH PHYSICS

Graduate Degree Programs
Georgia Institute of Technology, 32
National Technological University, 49

HIGHER EDUCATION

Individual Courses
Texas Tech University, 109
See also EDUCATION; TEACHER EDUCATION

HIGH SCHOOL ADVANCED PLACEMENT

Individual Courses
Ball State University, 4

HUMANITIES. *SEE* LIBERAL ARTS/GENERAL STUDIES

HUMAN RESOURCE DEVELOPMENT AND MANAGEMENT

Graduate Degree Programs
Indiana State University, 37
Utah State University, 166

MANAGEMENT; QUALITY
ASSURANCE AND
MANAGEMENT; RESOURCE
MANAGEMENT; RURAL
DEVELOPMENT; SOLID WASTE
MANAGEMENT TECHNOLOGY;
TECHNOLOGY AND
MANAGEMENT

MANAGEMENT/COMPUTER SCIENCE

Certificate Programs
New York University, 56

MANAGEMENT/ENGINEERING. *SEE* ENGINEERING MANAGEMENT

MANAGEMENT OF TECHNOLOGY.
SEE TECHNOLOGY AND
MANAGEMENT

MANUFACTURING SYSTEMS ENGINEERING

Graduate Degree Programs
Florida Atlantic University, 27
National Technological
University, 49
Rensselaer Polytechnic Institute, 75
University of Nebraska–Lincoln, 147

Certificate Programs
Rensselaer Polytechnic Institute, 75

MARKETING

Individual Courses
University of Maryland University
College, 140

MATERIALS SCIENCE AND ENGINEERING

Graduate Degree Programs
National Technological
University, 49
Rensselaer Polytechnic Institute, 75

Certificate Programs
Rensselaer Polytechnic Institute, 75

MATHEMATICS

Individual Courses
New Jersey Institute of
Technology, 54
See also STATISTICS

MECHANICAL ENGINEERING

Graduate Degree Programs
Colorado State University, 19
Florida Atlantic University, 27
Florida State University, 29
Georgia Institute of Technology, 32
Mary Washington College, 45
Oklahoma State University, 61
Old Dominion University, 63
Purdue University, 70
Rensselaer Polytechnic Institute, 75
Southern Methodist University, 96
University of Colorado at
Boulder, 122
University of Illinois at Urbana-
Champaign, 133
University of Nebraska–Lincoln, 147
University of South Carolina, 157

Undergraduate Degree Programs
Old Dominion University, 63

Certificate Programs
Rensselaer Polytechnic Institute, 75

MECHANICS

Graduate Degree Programs
University of Illinois at Urbana-
Champaign, 133

MEDICAL TECHNOLOGY

Undergraduate Degree Programs
University of North Dakota, 153

MENTAL HEALTH. *SEE* COMMUNITY MENTAL HEALTH

MICROCOMPUTER MANAGEMENT

Undergraduate Degree Programs
College of Great Falls, 16

MICROELECTRONICS MANUFACTURING

Graduate Degree Programs
Rensselaer Polytechnic Institute, 75

See also FOOD SCIENCE; TOURISM AND HOSPITALITY

ROBOTICS AND AUTOMATION
Certificate Programs
  Rensselaer Polytechnic Institute, 75

RURAL DEVELOPMENT
Undergraduate Degree Programs
  University of Alaska, Fairbanks, 114

SAFETY. *SEE* ENVIRONMENTAL HEALTH AND SAFETY; OCCUPATIONAL SAFETY MANAGEMENT

SCHOOL COUNSELING. *SEE* COUNSELING

SCIENCES
Individual Courses
  University of Maryland University College, 140
  See also APPLIED ARTS AND SCIENCE; CHEMISTRY; ENVIRONMENTAL HEALTH AND SAFETY; HEALTH PHYSICS; MATHEMATICS; NUCLEAR SCIENCE; PHYSICS

SOCIAL SCIENCES
Graduate Degree Programs
  Syracuse University, 105

Undergraduate Degree Programs
  Kansas State University, 41
  University of Wyoming, 164
  Washington State University, 169
  See also BEHAVIORAL AND SOCIAL SCIENCES; ECONOMICS; GEOGRAPHY; HUMAN SERVICES; LIBERAL ARTS/GENERAL STUDIES; SOCIOLOGY; STATISTICS

SOCIAL WORK
Undergraduate Degree Programs
  University of Alaska, Fairbanks, 114
  University of North Dakota, 153
Individual Courses
  Chadron State College, 15

College of Great Falls, 16
Colorado State University, 19
Portland State University, 69
University of Alaska, Fairbanks, 114
University of North Dakota, 153
University of South Carolina, 157
University of Wisconsin–Madison, 162
University of Wyoming, 164
Utah State University, 166
West Virginia University, 171
Wilfrid Laurier University, 172
See also HUMAN SERVICES

SOCIOLOGY
Undergraduate Degree Programs
  College of Great Falls, 16
  Wilfrid Laurier University, 172

Individual Courses
  New York Institute of Technology, 55

SOFTWARE ENGINEERING
Graduate Degree Programs
  National Technological University, 49
  Rochester Institute of Technology, 82
  University of Colorado at Boulder, 122

SOLID WASTE MANAGEMENT TECHNOLOGY
Certificate Programs
  Rochester Institute of Technology, 82

SPACE STUDIES
Individual Courses
  University of Colorado at Colorado Springs, 128

SPECIAL EDUCATION
Graduate Degree Programs
  University of Kentucky, 137
Certificate Programs
  San Jose State University, 94
  University of Calgary, 119
  University of Kentucky, 137